The Stardust of Yesterday

Boyd Gaming commissioned this painting by famed artist LeRoy Neiman to celebrate the final year of the Stardust and its 48 years of history. Neiman's long fascination with Las Vegas sports and gaming has been reflected in his work for Playboy *and other magazines.*

The Stardust of Yesterday

Reflections on a Las Vegas Legend

By Heidi Knapp Rinella ✦ Edited by Mike Weatherford

Foreword by Siegfried & Roy

Stephens Press
Las Vegas

ISBN-10: 1-932173-70-6
ISBN-13: 9781-932173-703

Credits
Editor: Mike Weatherford
Art Director: Jesse Dunaway
Publishing Coordinator: Stacey Fott
Front Cover Photographer: Larry Hanna
Jacket Designer: Chris Wheeler

CIP Data Available

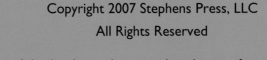
STEPHENS
PRESS, LLC
A Stephens Media Group Company

A Stephens Media Company
Post Office Box 1600
Las Vegas, NV 89125-1600
www.stephenspress.com

Printed in Hong Kong

Dedication

From 1958 to 2006, strong bonds of friendship were forged between the men and women employed at the Stardust and the people who made the resort their favorite vacation destination. The harmony resulting from these relationships made the Stardust a special place to work and visit. This book is dedicated to all of the loyal and gracious employees and guests who made the Stardust a Las Vegas legend.

Line art that decorated a champagne and wine menu from Café Continental, as the showroom was known in the early days.

Contents

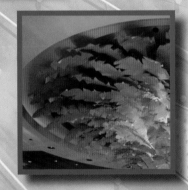

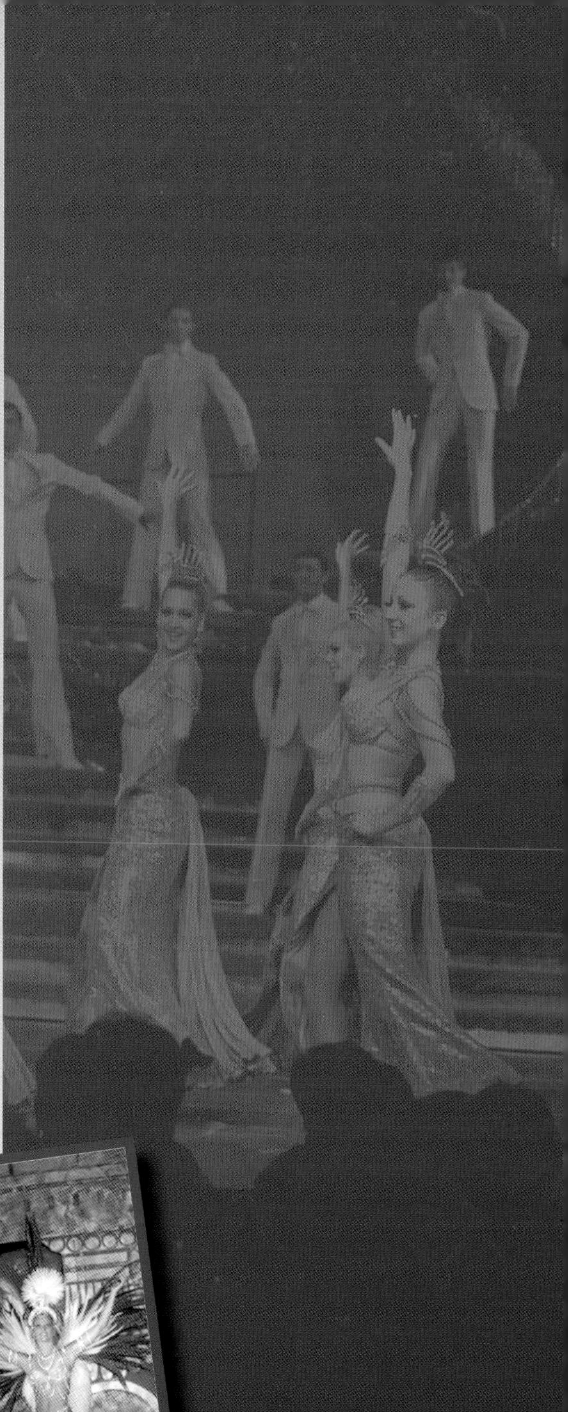

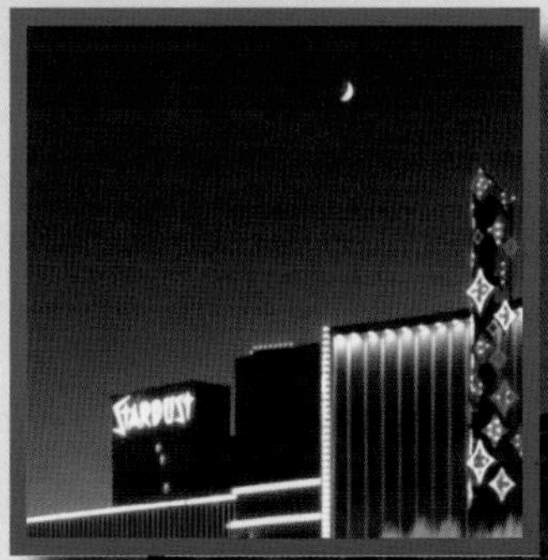

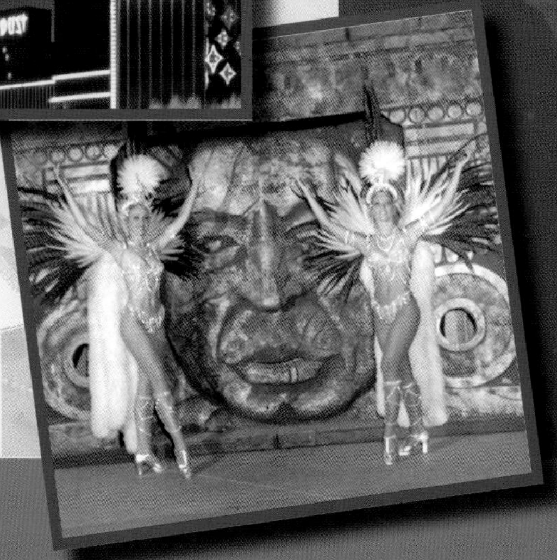

Foreword

LIDO DE PARIS
Starring
SIEGFRIED & ROY
Superstars of Magic

We were young together.

That's how we like to think of the Stardust. It was our performing home for six years and they were some of the most exciting years for all three of us.

It was 1970. Las Vegas had bloomed into a glittering neon oasis, a place where the famous and infamous mingled. Up and down The Strip, each night was like an elaborate production show, with visitors from around the world dressing up to play their part.

And the Stardust dazzled like no other.

We were brought to Las Vegas to star in Donn Arden's *Lido de Paris*. It was a glamorous stage production, brought to the Stardust by Frank Sennes, and our role lasted all of 15 minutes. At first, the thought of two German boys finding a home in Las Vegas was impossible to us. But the city, and the Stardust's general managers, Al Sachs and Herb Tobman, welcomed us with arms as wide as the desert itself. The Stardust was known for originality and taking chances and was always one step ahead of the others.

Here's a part of history not many people know: The first time Siegfried & Roy made a tiger disappear was on stage at the Stardust. Thankfully, we also knew how to make that same tiger appear again, or we wouldn't have lasted long.

We played at the Stardust until 1973, and then returned to headline *Lido* in 1978, our names on the giant marquee and lumps in our throat on opening night. We played 15 shows a week and would have played more. We broke the mold that said magicians couldn't be stars in Las Vegas, and the Stardust made it possible.

We'd go on to have separate but successful

LIDO DE PARIS
Starring
SIEGFRIED & ROY
Superstars
of
Magic

their dream gives that same chance to new ideas. From the land beneath the Stardust will come a spectacular new resort that will bring the same sense of wonder that the Stardust did a half-century ago.

But the memories of the Stardust, memories we share with those who worked and played there, are permanent. Many of them appear in these pages. Memories, after all, are not tigers or elephants. Even we can't make those disappear.

Magically,

Siegfried & Roy

futures, the Stardust and us. We moved down the block a ways, while the Stardust remained right where it was, one of the original, defining resorts on the Strip.

But Las Vegas is a city in constant evolution. New resorts fill the Strip today, new entertainment fills the theaters and we celebrate it all. The same spirit that gave two magicians from Germany a chance to live

Siegfried, left, and Roy on the red carpet for the premiere of Cirque du Soleil's Love *at The Mirage on June 28, 2006.*

11

Acknowledgments

Preserving the legacy of the legendary Stardust Hotel & Casino is a daunting responsibility and this book would not have been possible without the contributions of numerous individuals and organizations.

Bill Boyd, CEO and chairman of Boyd Gaming Corporation, supported this project from its inception and also offered his invaluable memories and insight in a personal interview.

Jim Seagrave, the Stardust's vice president of marketing and advertising, searched through the Stardust archives for memorabilia to bring this book to life. Jim was the first and staunchest champion of *The Stardust of Yesterday* and his assistance is deeply appreciated.

Many people shared their remembrances and personal stories of their Stardust experiences, including Len and Jill Rader, Carol Geraci, Shirley Brancucci, Lucille Waughsmith, George Havlik, Donald Fiscus, Ursula Stehn, Larry Seely, Akee Levin, Sue Kim, John Messana, Rena Warden and Fluff Le Coque. Thank you all.

The *Las Vegas Sun* and the *Las Vegas Review-Journal* news articles, photos and advertisements help tell the Stardust story from the perspective of the era. Some of those articles have been reproduced with generous permission.

The images — photos, illustrations, blueprints, artifacts, promotional materials, menus, postcards, show programs, advertisements and other memorabilia — illustrate the Stardust's legend. Larry Hanna's artistic manipulation of the venerable Stardust sign reflects the excitement of "old Las Vegas."

Darrin Bush of the Las Vegas News Bureau was the source of many archival photos. Photographer Shelly Donahue is responsible for the contemporary images of the property and long-time employees. Tonya Harvey took the studio shots of costumes and props. Many images also came from the *Las Vegas Review-Journal* archives and R-J photographers Isaac Brekken, Craig Moran and Jeff Scheid.

The glamour and glitz of the Stardust heyday is personified in the book jacket designed by Chris Wheeler. A mammoth task fell to book designer Jesse Dunaway to sort through the hundreds of images and fit them to the text. Jesse literally worked 24/7 (how Vegas!) to meet our impossible deadlines while creating a book that truly represents the Stardust legend and what it meant to generations of guests and staff.

Finally, my friend and editor, Mike Weatherford, entertainment reporter and columnist for the *Las Vegas Review-Journal* and author of *Cult Vegas: The Weirdest! The Wildest! The*

Swingin'est Town on Earth, who is a fount of knowledge on all things Vegas. Mike worked tirelessly to help unearth the most interesting facts and unique images and relentlessly pursued the dates and details of long-past events.

The Stardust legend lives on . . .

— Heidi Knapp Rinella

13

Introduction

When the Stardust Resort and Casino made its Las Vegas Strip debut on July 2, 1958, the world took notice.

The international media took note that the Stardust was the world's largest hotel (1,032 rooms) and had the world's largest electric sign (5,832 square feet).

Also generating attention was its primary entertainment attraction, *Lido de Paris*, a breathtaking stage show with futuristic special effects, spectacular costumes and elegant showgirls from Paris.

Visitors to Las Vegas were captivated by the block-long neon galaxy of planets and stars that framed the entrance and created an irresistible invitation to see what was inside.

From the beginning, the Stardust exceeded every guest's expectations. Throughout its remarkable history, it offered a dazzling variety of amenities, such as a world-class motor sports raceway, a championship golf course and rodeo grounds. The fascinating list also included a drive-in movie, an RV park, a bus depot and museum that chronicled the history of gambling. It seemed that the Stardust was always looking for new ways to please its guests beyond its luxurious accommodations, exceptional restaurants, electrifying casino games and spacious swimming pools.

As a young man, I spent many memorable evenings with my friends watching wonderful entertainers such as the Kim Sisters and the Royal Irish Showband perform in the Stardust Lounge. It was always a special treat to enjoy the cuisine in unique restaurants such as Aku Aku and Moby Dick.

When Boyd Gaming acquired the Stardust in 1985

our company instantly achieved new levels of prestige. For us, to be entrusted with this legendary resort was a cherished responsibility and a labor of love. Adding a 32-story tower and a 65,000-square-foot convention complex to the Stardust was one of our most satisfying achievements. We will forever be honored to have been associated with such a vital component of our city's history.

The *Stardust Of Yesterday* is a line from one of the most recorded songs of all time, *Star Dust*. The lyrics were written in 1929 by Mitchell Parrish to a tune composed two years earlier by Hoagy Carmichael. A Las Vegas legend maintains that this romantic song inspired the builders of the hotel to give their masterpiece a name that suggests a place where visitors can leave their everyday cares behind them for a while. "Stardust" proved to be a perfect name.

This book will take you on a mesmerizing pictorial journey from a burgeoning desert town that was just starting to make a name for itself

to a vibrant 21st century metropolis that continually commands global attention.

The Stardust will always remain a symbol of the glamour and hospitality that has allowed our city to grow and prosper. Most responsible for the popularity and success of this great resort are the thousands of talented and dedicated employees who served our guests.

This extraordinary team unfailingly treated our guests and each other with respect, dignity, compassion and friendliness. This book serves as a tribute to their incomparable contributions.

— William S. Boyd
Chairman & CEO
Boyd Gaming

15

An Inspiration

A gambler has a big idea but doesn't live to see the jackpot

Dust

William S. "Bill" Boyd's first Stardust memories are of a dusty, wind-swept construction site circa 1956. Work on the project had been halted when the first owners ran out of money.

"I remember driving by it for a long time half-built," said Boyd, today chairman and CEO of Boyd Gaming Corporation. "The story was the guy who started it had a heart attack shooting craps at the Desert Inn."

That guy would be Tony Cornero, one of a string of … ahem … *colorful* characters associated with the Stardust during the first half of its life.

Cornero (whose birth name was Stralla) had owned two gambling ships, the S.S. Rex and

TONY CORNERO STRALLA

Tony Cornero had big ideas for the Stardust, but they included only a small outdoor sign in this pre-construction rendering. Alas, Cornero wouldn't survive to see the finished product or the supersized, iconic sign that eventually defined the casino.

Paying respects

The city's two newspapers, the Las Vegas Review-Journal *and* Las Vegas Sun, *always celebrated their contrasts in political opinion and news judgement. This was illustrated in their reporting of Tony Cornero's death in 1955, only a few years into the newspaper rivalry.*

The Review-Journal news account of August 1, 1955, kept references to the Stardust project at a minimum:

Cornero, Gambler, Succumbs

Funeral services for Anthony Stralla, better known in Las Vegas as Tony Cornero, who died yesterday morning of a heart attack, will be held in Los Angeles sometime later this week, it was reported today.

The body left Las Vegas at 6 o'clock this morning enroute for the Southern California community where the rites will be under the direction of Edwards Brothers' mortuary. Cornero was preparing to open his new Stardust Hotel on the Strip when he was stricken.

The gambler was one of the most colorful figures in the industry. He was 55 years of age and is credited by many old-time Las Vegans as being the "father" of the resort hotel industry in this area through the construction of the Meadows casino and hotel here in 1932. He and his brothers, Frank and Louis, constructed the establishment on East Charleston about the time Boulder Dam was under way and operated it, with varying success, until about 1940.

Cornero made and lost three or four fortunes. During the time of the construction of the Meadows, he was in McNeil's Island federal penitentiary serving a term for rum running and, after his release, came to Las Vegas to aid his brothers in the operation of the Meadows.

Since 1924, Cornero, then known in gambling circles as "The Admiral," battled stubbornly with law enforcement agencies, including his days as a run runner for "the carriage trade."

It was estimated that during his gambling club ventures he was grossing $6,000,000 per year. His greatest three-day profit came from the operation of the Lux when he picked up $173,000 before the craft was padlocked by Federal Judge John O'Connor.

The Sun *of that day was more bullish on the Stardust project, right from the first paragraph:*

Tony Cornero Stricken While Gambling, Dies

Anthony (Tony Cornero) Stralla, promoter of the most ambitious resort hotel in Ls Vegas history — the Stardust — died yesterday, before it opened, and his brother Louis has been elected to succeed him. . . .

The shrewd veteran of California's celebrated gambling boat "wars" of the 1930s and 1940s had raised $10,000,000 from more than 2,800 stockholders to build the Sta-

rust, which is scheduled to open September 1.

Cornero battled great odds in his successful fight to finish the Stardust, which was only a stepping stone to his ultimate goal: a lavish, $20,000,000 resort here which was his dream for the future.

Cornero planned to pay everly cent of Stardust profits to his stockholders, to build confidence in the public for his super resort project to come. He personally held 60 per cent of the Stardust.

TONY CORNERO STRALLA

★ ★ ★ ★ ★ ★ ★ ★

Cornero, Gambler, Succumbs

Funeral services for Anthony Stralla, better known in Las Vegas as Tony Cornero, who died yesterday morning of a heart attack, will be held in Los Angeles sometime later this week, it was reported here today.

The body left Las Vegas at 6 o'clock this morning enroute for the Southern California community, where the rites will be under the direction of Edwards Brothers' mortuary. Cornero was preparing to open his new Stardust Hotel on the Strip when he was stricken.

An inquest will be held in Las Vegas this afternoon at 5 30 o'clock under the direction of Deputy Coroner Glenn E Bodell.

Cornero, who had suffered from heart trouble for the past several years, died in his room at the Desert Inn shortly before 11 o'clock after he was stricken while standing in the casino watching the gambling. He was rushed to the room and a resuscitator squad was summoned, and they worked over him for about half an hour without success.

Doctors Aid

Dr. Alfred S. Erlich, of Los Angeles, one of Cornero's partners in the hotel venture, and Dr. G. W. Fineman, a guest in the hotel, were summoned to assist Cornero when he slumped onto the floor, but their ministrations were of no avail.

The gambler was one of the most colorful figures in the industry. He was 55 years of age and is credited by many old-time Las Vegans as being the "father" of the resort hotel industry in this area through the construction of the Meadows casino and hotel here in 1932. He and his brothers. Frank and Louis, constructed the establishment on East Charleston about the time Boulder Dam was under way and operated it, with varying success, until about 1940.

Cornero made and lost three or four fortunes. During the time of the construction of the Meadows. he was in McNeil's Island federal penitentiary serving a term for rum running and, after his release, came to Las Vegas to aid his brothers in the operation of the Meadows.

When the resort folded. Cornero went to Southern California where

The original design of the Stardust was piece- meal, with each func- tion designed separate- ly without regard to the sum of the parts.

S.S. Tango, which ferried 1930s-era gamblers by motorboat from Depression-insulated Southern California to the Pacific waters just outside the 3-mile limit. The story — in an era filled with rich stories — was that Cornero lost the Tango in a poker game, and the Rex was seized by authorities annoyed by the blatantly illegal operation.

But the ships weren't Cornero's first entrepreneurial forays into the world of gaming. In Southern Nevada, he and his brothers had built the Meadows Casino and Hotel in 1931. It was located outside the Las Vegas city limits, allegedly to avoid the prying eyes of the city council. They sold the hotel operations a few months later. A few months after that, the hotel was destroyed by a fire that was allegedly ignored by City of Las Vegas firefighters, because, after all, it was outside the city limits.

The casino closed the following year.

Tony Tries Again

Having twice seen his fortunes rise and fall, Cornero tried another Las Vegas venture, but soon lost his license. Decamping to Southern California, he considered gaming opportunities in Mexico, only to be persuaded otherwise when one day, he answered his door to four bullets in the stomach.

So, back to Las Vegas it was.

Despite a haphazard design concept, the buildings were constructed to last, with extensive use of concrete block and steel.

23

Bullets and busts couldn't dissuade Cornero. He dreamed of building a hotel and casino that were, as his freshly minted business cards promised, the "largest and most luxurious in the world."

He bought 40 acres on the Strip in 1953, but ran out of money. Pretty soon, business cards weren't the only thing Cornero was printing up. Desperate to raise funds to build his Stardust, he sold shares in the project without bothering to work with the Securities and Exchange Commission. Thousands of investors were bilked. And as for the pesky detail of a gaming license? Well, since Tony's record dated to a conviction for rumrunning during Prohibition — and considering the guy's track record to date — the Nevada Gaming Commission was no doubt highly amused. Cornero eventually struck a

management agreement with Milton "Farmer" Page, who held a license as owner of the Pioneer Club.

The Stardust was almost, but not quite, a reality by 1955, when Cornero appealed for support from Moe Dalitz and Meyer Lansky. The Cleveland mobsters operated the Desert Inn through their United Hotels front, and they were eager to enlarge their Las Vegas footprint. But there were plenty of unforeseen expenses — maybe a few that weren't exactly normal business expenses — and money just seemed to vanish

The dusty, windswept site of the Stardust would stay that way for several years, as various obstacles blocked completion.

like a desert mirage. As loan after loan stacked up, Cornero eventually was into United Hotels for more than $4 million. He went back to the well one last time for money to open the Stardust at 9:30 a.m. on July 31. His fatal heart attack occurred at a Desert Inn craps table less than two hours later.

Coincidence? It's hard to say. Cornero's body was taken to a casino office. The sheriff wasn't called until nearly two hours later. The glass from which he had been drinking disappeared and no autopsy was performed. The death became another of the intriguing mysteries that dot the history of Las Vegas.

WELCOME! WELCOME! the star-spangled STARDUST

ASTONISHING! EXCITING! THRILLING!

with the world-famed "LIDO DE PARIS REVUE" *a history making entertainment event in Las Vegas!*

Wilbur Clark's DESERT INN

The expansive, albeit somewhat utilitarian vision of the Stardust is evident in this aerial photo showing its 1,032 rooms laid out in five symmetrical rows of motel units. The old Royal Nevada, at left in the photo, contrasts the more modest but architecturally graceful designs of the pre-Stardust casinos.

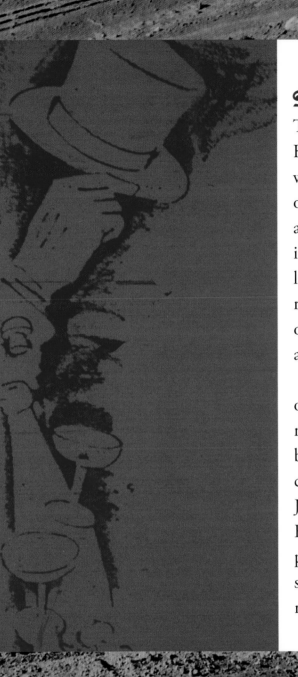

The Shutdown

The project's troubles continued when United Hotels took over and labor disputes led to a work stoppage. There was a lot of construction on the Strip during this period — the Riviera and the Dunes opened in 1955, the Hacienda in 1956 and the Tropicana in 1957 — and labor was short anyway. The Stardust went into receivership after an investor filed a lawsuit over missing funds, and the project languished another two years.

Various groups vied to bring the Stardust out of bankruptcy and finally open it as the newest star on the Las Vegas Strip. In 1957, a bankruptcy judge considered five proposals, choosing one early the next year backed by Jack Factor, brother of cosmetics icon Max Factor. Jack's wife, Rella, became the official president of the Stardust, but the Factors were simply backers for Dalitz & Co., who would run the place (and who would officially assume control in September 1958).

Work resumed, and the money flowed once again. And flowed, and flowed. Cornero's architectural guidelines apparently had been about as flexible as his attitude toward the law. The place he had been building turned out to be rather offbeat in its design and construction; revisions were required. More than $1 million reportedly was poured into the showroom alone to ready it for the demands of the imported *Lido de Paris.*

"It is likely that the Stardust was initially designed largely by the engineer or contractor," architecture critic Alan Hess writes in his book *Viva Las Vegas: After-Hours Architecture.* "The design was a collection of individual functions (motel wings, casino, showroom) without an overall concept or image."

But on July 2, 1958, the Stardust — and a new star for the Strip — was born.

Tomorrow  at High Noon...

will be the most exciting
moment in your life!

Gala opening of "The Strip's"
most magnificent hotel~

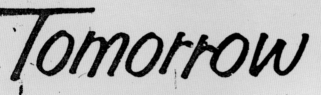

TOMORROW!
GALA PRESS PREVIEW

An "invitation only" event
for press, radio,
television and motion
picture celebrities

THURSDAY—JULY 2
GRAND OPENING!
8:15 p.m.—Midnight

Two brilliant "FIRST
NIGHT" Shows!

Nightly:
8:15 p.m. and 12 Midnight

Saturdays:
8:45 p.m. to Midnight - 2:15 a.m.

EXTRA! George Jessel - Opening Night Master of Ceremonies!

When Stars Are Bright

A casino trades on volume and a sign as big as the galaxy

Mass Production

If anything attributable to Cornero survived, it was his populist vision. The Stardust would point the way to the city's future for years to come by embracing "mass" as well as "class." The Sands or Desert Inn could have the high rollers. The Stardust would deal in volume and make a profit from middle America. It was touted as the world's largest hotel, with 1,032 rooms, and the two-story motel units behind the casino were lined up "like boxcars at the freight yard," Hess noted. The 16,500-square-foot casino was easily the largest in the state (and, considering the scarcity of gaming in the United States in those days, probably the country as well). Its Big Dipper swimming pool was the state's largest, at 105 feet long.

And how was all this packaged and sold? "It had one of the great signs on the Strip," Boyd said.

While the original architectural concept for the hotel-casino called for a modestly sized "Tony Cornero's Stardust" neon banner, the finished resort's hallmark would be its iconic sign and, in true Las Vegas fashion, lots and lots of lights. Backed by a stylized

Opposite page: The Stardust drafted show-girls for a publicity photo to capitalize on the hotel's opening on the Fourth of July weekend.

West themes, the Stardust offered nothing less than a panorama of the solar system that exploded beyond the edges of the building."

The casino was intended as a place for Everyman. But there was much about the Stardust that was special — particularly its *Lido de Paris* stage show — and once it was built, more than Everyman came.

"I was impressed that most of the vehicles (in the parking lot) were Cadillacs, Lincolns — high-end cars," said Larry Seely, who joined the Stardust as a bellman just two months later and continued to work there until the resort closed.

A Different Era

The early days of the Strip were very different from the city today.

"They used to have dinner shows," Seely said. He saw plenty of "white ermine coats, short and long furs. People were dressed up and they all looked nice. It was a chance to get dressed up without going to a wedding or a funeral."

And the golden-age Strip was far from the

Publicity materials for the new casino touted the outdoor sign's 129-ton weight and bragged that "84 gallons of automotive enamels" were used in its construction. The 16-foot globe sported "a restless 'sputnik' in constant motion around it."

representation of the galaxy that practically covered the entire façade of the place, it announced the Stardust not once but twice, with a planet between the two. This was indeed the new center of the universe.

"It became the Stardust's architecture by default, yet was no accident," Hess notes in his book. "Freed from architectural convention, from sophistication, even from exotic and Old

A postcard for the new hotel boasted of "some 40 acres of gardens and architectural splendor" designed to meet visitors' "every need and comfort."

The Stardust

Show Time

STARDUST

July 11, 1963 cca

LAS VEGAS, NEVADA

ON THE "STRIP"

REgent 5-6111

PLEASE PRESENT WHEN REGISTERING

7-28
8-2   PRYSTUPA,M.J.,M/M   1-T
cca   c/o Fairmont Hotel $8-14
To: San Francisco   noon
           California

All reservations are made subject to strikes, failure of guests to vacate, or causes or conditions beyond our control.

Acknowledged by   cca

This will confirm and thank you for your room reservation. Accommodations will be set aside as follows:

Date of Arr. **July 28**   Date of Dep. **Aug. 2**
Day **Sunday**   Time of Ar.
Accommodations: Deposit
1 twin bedded room
$8-14

Please Note:

Reservations are made in name as shown and are not transferable. Rooms will be held only until 7 p.m. unless otherwise notified. In case of cancellation please notify us immediately. You will be accommodated as soon after arrival as possible subject to availability of accommodations. We appreciate your reservation and look forward to having you with us.

Cordially,
STARDUST

Requested By **direct**

Credit Card No.

A "twin-bedded room" at the Stardust could be had for as little as $8 in 1963, which prompted some guests at other hotels to rent rooms there just to be able to buy tickets to Lido de Paris.

Bare desert still surrounds it, but by 1965 the Stardust had added a nine-story room tower, a new outdoor sign along the Strip and a new façade replacing the old galaxy front.

densely packed, 24-hour bustle of today. When the Stardust opened, its nearby neighbors were the Desert Inn, which opened in 1950, just down the road to the southeast; the Sands, which opened in 1952, a little farther south; and the Riviera, which opened in 1955, almost directly across the street to the north.

There were a few other casinos, but not much else. As Jill Rader, who arrived from England in 1959 as a cast member of the *Lido de Paris*, remembers, "There was sand between each hotel."

"In those days, you could see the heat waves rising off the desert," Seely said. "When the wind blew the sand, you couldn't see the Riviera."

As for the Flamingo, "We used to say you had to take a real ride to get there," Boyd remembers with a chuckle.
"Most people thought you lived in a hotel," said former Stardust showgirl Rena Warden. "They didn't believe there were churches in Las Vegas."

Horsemans Park, *lower left, hosted rodeos and horse shows that helped keep the* western spirit of Nevada *alive on the Strip for a few more years. Ed Sullivan, below, broadcast his popular Sunday "really big shoe" from the showroom in 1962.*

39

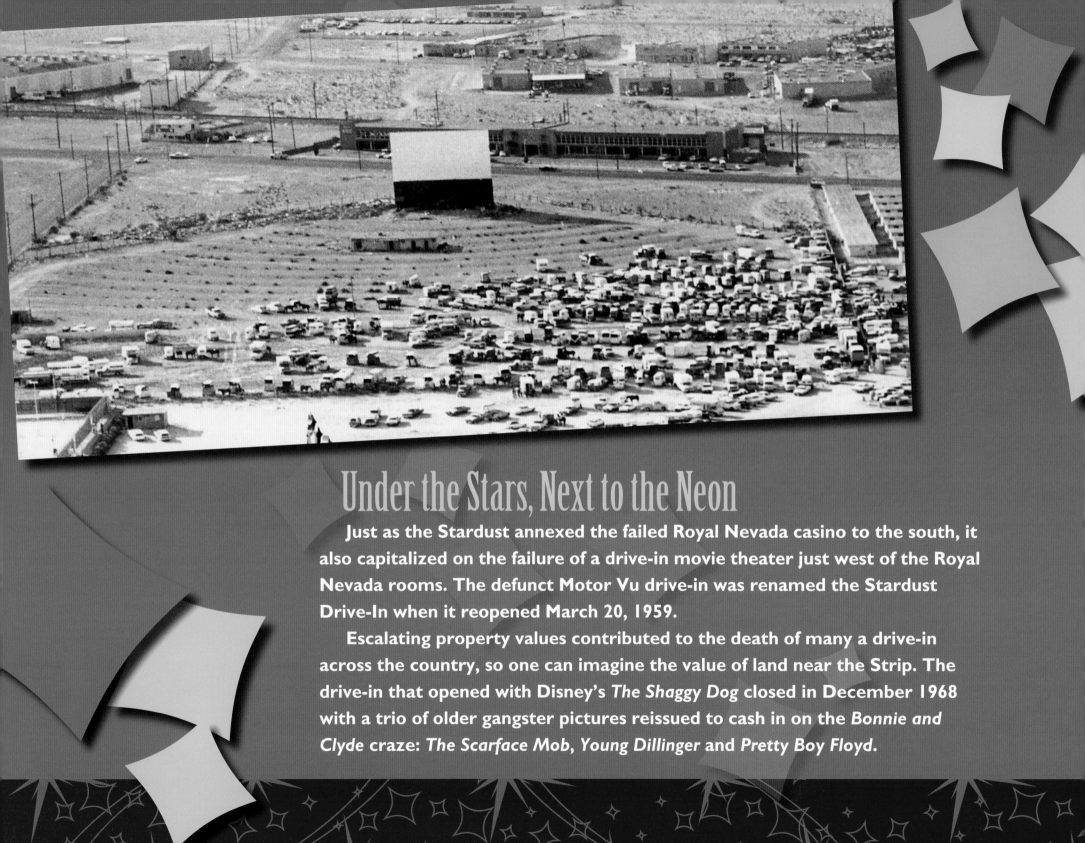

Under the Stars, Next to the Neon

Just as the Stardust annexed the failed Royal Nevada casino to the south, it also capitalized on the failure of a drive-in movie theater just west of the Royal Nevada rooms. The defunct Motor Vu drive-in was renamed the Stardust Drive-In when it reopened March 20, 1959.

Escalating property values contributed to the death of many a drive-in across the country, so one can imagine the value of land near the Strip. The drive-in that opened with Disney's *The Shaggy Dog* closed in December 1968 with a trio of older gangster pictures reissued to cash in on the *Bonnie and Clyde* craze: *The Scarface Mob*, *Young Dillinger* and *Pretty Boy Floyd*.

The Aku Aku tiki gods were the forerunner of today's oversized gimmicks — volcanos, pirate ships, etc. — designed to lure motorists from the highway.

A Cash-ready Town

"When I started, chips were good anywhere," Seely said. He frequently was tipped in chips, and sometimes, "they might've wanted to drop one or two and they dropped three." Easy come, easy go. Now, Seely figures, he's tipped maybe one chip a week.

Shirley Brancucci, a cocktail server who became the city's first female baccarat dealer at the Stardust, remembers when chips could be used at the dry cleaner and pizzeria, and other casinos honored them interchangeably. The old joke had it that in church, certain friars were assigned to collect the chips and cash them in. Those would be the "chip monks."

And silver dollars were much more freely used than they are now. Seely can remember having to cash in his silver dollars part-way through a shift, because their weight was pulling his pants down.

A Time of Growth

Soon after its opening, the Stardust continued to grow. The shuttered Royal Nevada next door to the south was a rare failure during the 1950s boom. The Stardust annexed the property, adding its motel wings and swimming pool in 1959 and turning the casino proper into the Stardust Convention Center.

Through the '60s, the Stardust established an ever-more-notable spot in Las Vegas, even as management continued to be somewhat shady. Dalitz and his partners retained a majority interest. The various members of the management team included one with seven aliases on file with the Los Angeles Police Department and another who allegedly had been an associate of Al Capone.

But they knew what the customer wanted. The drive-in was so successful that it was expanded in 1960.

That same year, the new restaurant Aku Aku capitalized on the tiki and Polynesian craze launched by Trader Vic's. A giant "tiki god" posted at the outisde door became a hard-to-miss landmark that would herald the Strip's penchant for architectural kitsch.

The Stardust Country Club, four miles from the property to the east, hosted numerous tournaments that brought the big names in golf and accompanying national attention.

Much the same way, the Stardust International Raceway brought high-profile races to a track west of the property. And the *Lido* was changed each year with a new "Direct from Paris!" edition to ensure continued interest.

Ed Sullivan broadcast his popular Sunday-evening TV variety show from the showroom in 1962. A nine-story hotel tower was added in 1964, challenging the height of the Riviera across the street. Cassius Clay (the future Muhammad Ali) trained at the Stardust Convention Center for his November 1965 bout with Floyd Patterson. Stardust Horsemans Park opened on the hotel-casino grounds in 1967.

If the multiple recreational offerings in present-day Las Vegas are impressive, consider

The details behind these Las Vegas News Bureau *publicity photos have been lost to time. But the photo above and those of the dancer on the artillery piece, above right and on the following two pages, most likely were from a ceremony welcoming a military unit to town.*

The Royal Nevada

The Royal Nevada, which would become the Stardust Convention Center in 1958, had one of the shortest life spans in Las Vegas Strip history. But its few months of existence would encompass three firsts.

One involved its original ownership; Missourian Roberta May Simon, who held a 10-percent stake in the casino-hotel, was the first woman to hold a Nevada gaming license.

One had to do with Las Vegas' finest bring-'em-in-and-take-their-money tradition; the Royal Nevada is said to be the first local property to introduce all-you-can-eat prime rib at its Chuckwagon, in August 1957. The price: $1.50.

And the other ... well, we'll get to that later.

Topped by a Gulliver-sized crown trimmed in neon, the Lilliputian resort came to life April 19, 1955, during heady times in Las Vegas. The Strip was booming. The Royal Nevad's debut was book-ended by the births of the Riviera, which opened April 20, and the Dunes, which opened May 23.

All of that action drew the attention of the national press, and the Royal Nevada took full advantage of the spotlight. Its lounge hosted a number of well-known en-

The Royal Nevada room wings and pool remained an oasis of old-Vegas tranquility until the final summer of the Stardust, when the rooms were closed ahead of the rest of the hotel. Repeat customers often would request a room in the Royal Nevada area, one of the last vestiges of 1950s construction that remained on the strip after 2000.

tertainers, including the Dukes of Dixieland — which, as it was less well known, included Liberace's brothers Frank and Fred. The showroom pioneered the concept of bringing shortened Broadway musicals to the Strip with a production of *Guys and Dolls*, which reunited its original Broadway stars, Robert Alda, Vivian Blaine and Sam Levene.

The excitement was to be short-lived. After a dispute with a union over back wages, the resort abruptly closed its doors the following January 1 after only eight months. A group of investors including Bill Miller, who had been the publicist for the Sahara, revived it as Bill Miller's Royal Nevada later that year. But the resort closed again in 1958, this time for good.

The Stardust next door bought the property and turned most of the showroom and casino space into the Stardust Convention Center. The motel building became the Pool Wing of the Stardust. The former Royal Nevada pool may have been more obscure than the Stardust's Big Dipper, but that probably didn't bother the savvier tourists who knew showgirls liked to swim nude there.

On, and that other first? That had to do with the Royal Nevada's demise. The real reasons are lost to history, but, this being Las Vegas, theories (and rumors) abound. Many

The departure of the Royal Nevada's signature crown was a more dignified send-off than The Amazing Colossal Man gave to a movie prop version of it in 1957.

said the Royal Nevada simply was a victim of a weak economy and overbuilding; this reportedly was the only time in Las Vegas history when the supply of hotel rooms outstripped the demand from guests. The Moulin Rouge, the integrated casino that opened in West Las Vegas the day after the Dunes, also was at least in part a victim of oversupply.

But there's another, more tantalizing story that surrounds the end of the Royal Nevada: that it was the only casino — definitely in Las Vegas, certainly in Nevada and, well, probably anywhere in the world — to be broken by gamblers.

A model touts the opening of Camperland in October 1972. The 150-space RV park was so successful that managers decided within three weeks to expand it.

that the sprawling grounds of the Stardust offered something for everyone during this period, including a supervised playground for the kiddies and horseback riding at Horsemans Park. There were conventions, trade shows and various awards ceremonies held on the property almost continually.

"You name it, I saw it," said Warden, who was with *Lido* from 1969 to 1979. "As a showgirl, you could donate your time. I did a helicopter convention because I wanted my boys to ride a helicopter."

In 1966, Howard Hughes was deep into his Las Vegas casino-buying orgy (he was eager to invest the funds stemming from his sale of Trans World Airlines) and made an offer for the Stardust. But he was tripped up by anti-trust regulations, since he already owned the Desert Inn,

Sands, Frontier, Silver Slipper and Castaways. The feds had decided enough was enough.

The Parvin-Dohrmann Corporation of Los Angeles (which had acquired the Aladdin the year before) was more successful, buying the Stardust in 1969. That was the same year Kirk Kerkorian opened the Las Vegas International (now the Las Vegas Hilton) on Paradise Road. With more than 1,500 rooms, it became the first property to eclipse the Stardust's claim to the most hotel rooms in the world, which it had held for 10 years.

But the Stardust wasn't down for the count. It added Camperland in 1972, and about the same time advertised that it had not one but two swimming pools, five restaurants and world-class tennis courts in addition to all of its other amenities.

The success of Camperland sealed the fate of Horsemans Park, which would be closed to add 250 spaces to the RV park. The bleachers, corrals and other portions of the park were donated to Dixie College in St. George, Utah.

The Purple Dusk

A guy with connections loses his grip and a corporation cleans up

Lefty Enters The Picture

The early 1970s also ushered in the era of Frank "Lefty" Rosenthal and Tony "The Ant" Spilotro as the next organized crime-related characters drawn to the Stardust. The reign of the Argent Corporation and the mob skimming of cash from its properties would earn the Stardust infamy in news headlines and, later, immortality through Nicholas Pileggi's book *Casino* and Martin Scorsese's 1995 movie of the same name.

Parvin-Dorhmann offshoot Recrion Corporation was trying to sell the place. Young Los Angeles developer Allen R. Glick had come to town in 1972 with the intention of tearing down the bankrupt Hacienda and turning the land into a mobile-home park, but decided it might be more profitable to operate the gambling hall.

Glick got his gaming license, and, as he told Pileggi in *Casino*, "There I was, at twenty-nine or thirty, chairman of a Las Vegas casino. Within a day, everyone in town had a deal for me."

One of those deals was a Lake Tahoe casino that had been foreclosed on by the Central States Teamster Pension Fund. That deal didn't work out for Glick, but through it he met Al Baron, assets manager for the fund. When Glick developed a subsequent office complex in Texas, he approached Baron and the Teamsters for financial backing.

Another of those deals involved the Stardust, plus the Fremont, which Recrion also owned. Glick went back to Baron, who tried to warn him off. But when Glick persisted, Baron put him in touch with Teamster trustees. By August 1974, Glick owned the Stardust, and the Chicago mob owned him. And Rosenthal, a skilled sports handicapper and Chicago native, was connected to them both.

Rosenthal had joined the Stardust as a floor man in 1971. A longtime professional gambler, he'd taken a casino job because his wife, former Tropicana showgirl Gerri McGee, wanted a "normal life," and running his own

Opposite page: Frank "Lefty" Rosenthal was unable to obtain a Nevada gaming license, but was the power behind the Stardust. Rosenthal's tumultous life was complicated by his marriage to former Tropicana showgirl Gerri, above.

Frank Rosenthal na... consultant at LV hotels

Argent Corporation has announced the appointment of casino executive Frank Rosenthal, to the office of executive consultant to the chairman of the board.

Allen R. Glick, president and chairman of the board of Argent, said Rosenthal would serve as the corporation's executive consultant for the Stardust and Fremont Hotels.

OCT 2 2 1974

Rosenthal will serve in a similar capacity with the Hacienda Hotel and the Airport Marina, set to open on the Strip early next year. Glick is a major owner of the latter properties.

Rosenthal, 45, a native to Chicago, has been prominent in the Las Vegas gaming industry for the past 10 years. He resides here with his wife Geri; son, Steve, 4½, and daughter, Stephanie, 1½.

The vital, new post being filled by Rosenthal will see him conferring with and recommending to Glick, "policies which will insure the integrity and standards of the resort-gaming industry and Argent Corporation."

Rosenthal brings with him the finest of credentials as a business management expert in the gaming industry. Until his recent appointment, he had served as coordinator of casino services for the Stardust Hotel, working closely with Stardust president Allan D. Sachs.

In naming Rosenthal to his new post, Glick said, "I feel extremely fortunate to have a man with Frank Rosenthal's qualifications working directly with me on establishing and carrying out general policies for all of our resorts. He has been a great credit to Nevada's gaming industry and is one of the most respected members of this thriving business community."

Rosenthal stated that he would be working closely with Sachs, James J. Hill, president of the Fremont Hotel and Eugene Fresch, executive vice-president in charge of operations for Argent.

"Our hotels have the strongest management staffs in the State of Nevada," Rosenthal said. "In addition to continuing to operate as smoothly and profitably as we have in the past, the Argent Corporation resorts will do everything possible to maintain the great respect enjoyed by all gaming industries throughout the world."

BOARD RECOMMENDS DENIAL OF ROSENTHAL LICENSE

Lefty Gets 'Thumbs Down'

CARSON CITY (UPI) — The State Gaming Control Board yesterday recommended denial of a Nevada gaming license for professional gambler Frank Rosenthal on grounds he was involved in two bribery attempts of college athletes in 1960.

Rosenthal sought to be director of Nevada operations for the Argent Corporation, which runs the Stardust and Fremont Hotel-Casinos in Las Vegas. The vote by the three-member board was unanimous.

Board member Jack Stratton said the state "cannot risk fixing the stamp of approval on Mr. Rosenthal." He said licensing of Rosenthal would reflect discredit on the state and the gaming industry.

The denial goes before the Nevada Gaming Commission, which meets here Jan. 22 for final action. The commission must have a unanimous vote of its five members to overturn the board.

Philip Hannifin, Chairman of the Board, said if the recommendation was upheld it would mean Rosenthal could not work in the industry.

The vote came after a two-day hearing in which Rosenthal was questioned extensively about his past arrest record, his associations with alleged members of the underworld and his work record.

Business leaders, friends and coworkers testified that Rosenthal, since coming to Las Vegas in 1968, has built a reputation for honesty, integrity, fairness and a strict conformity to state gaming regulations.

Hannifin said he always has to weigh the issue of a person who is capable against a bad reputation. He said state control agencies have strived to increase the standards of those who are licensed in Nevada in the last five years.

Hannifin said there was a question of credibility in this case. He said that to believe Rosenthal would mean he would have to disbelieve court records, responsible police officers and statements made by a young man under oath at the McClellan Senate Rackets Committee about an alleged bribe.

"I cannot disbelieve all of these people," Hannifin said.

Rosenthal s...

(Continued from Page 1)

better smarten up your son or you'll find your head in Chicago and your body in Chicago Heights."

Rosenthal said if he had paid off the police, they never would have showed up at his apartment to arrest him.

Hannifin said it was a "minor concern" if Rosenthal had been involved in illegal gaming, claiming everyone who had built the Nevada gaming industry had been engaged in some illegal gambling activity before coming here.

But he said he was especially concerned about allegations Rosenthal attempted to corrupt public officials with payoffs, in this case the North Bay Village Police, which he termed "abhorrent."

"This one really bothers me," said Hannifin, calling an end to the Wednesday session a short time later.

Hours before, Argent board chairman Allen R. Glick took the stand as Rosenthal's first witness, claiming the Control Board decision "will have resounding effects on this industry."

"Today we have a man on trial," said Glick, "on trial for his livelihood, reputation and right to work."

"Argent, myself and Frank have become targets of conjecture, innuendos and just plain malicious attacks," Glick told the three-member Control Board.

"To p...
circumst...
by the el...
interests o...
justice," sa...

"The poli...
influenced b...
man's career...

Glick was qu...
to say Mr. Ro...
absence?

"Absolutely co...

The Argent chie...
including 80-year-...
Stardust Hotel, whi...

Jaffe testified in a...
with Rosenthal abou...
said, "he (Rosenthal)...
Glick's business pa...
from the Argent dir...
ciplinarian," but sensi...
tions

Rosenthal show

By Jack Breger
R-J Staff Writer

CARSON CITY — Frank Rosenthal revealed here Wednesday he was arrested for illegal gambling in Florida because he would not work undercover for the Federal Bureau of Investigation.

He told the Gaming Control Board an FBI agent offered him immunity from arrest if he took the job, but he rejected the idea and ended in jail.

Rosenthal was before the Board to be licensed with Argent Corp.

which operates the Stardust, Fremont, Hacienda and Marina Hotel casinos.

The Board adjourned at 8 p.m. Wednesday and scheduled more testimony Thursday.

At the Wednesday session more than 15 witnesses testified to Rosenthal's good character and competency in his post as director of Nevada operations for Argent, which operates several Las Vegas resorts.

The last witness was Rosenthal who talked about his childhood while answering questions from Board Chairman Phil Hannifin, explained he had a terrible memory for dates and an inability to remember what year he graduated high school.

Rosenthal recalled how his mother gave him a $1.50 allowance in grade school and how he would save a dollar to buy parlay tickets at 50 cents a piece at the corner drugstore on weekend.

He discussed dropping out of junior college and joining the military police combat unit during the Korean War.

Rosenthal said he continued to wager on sports events as part...

OCT 1 1 1980 SUN   Saturday, October 11, 1980   LAS VEGAS

Rosenthal Denies 'War' With Spilotro Near...

By JEFFREY M. GERMAN
SUN Staff Writer

Ex-gaming figure Frank Rosenthal Friday denied allegations in the SUN that a rift between the former Stardust Hotel executive and reputed mobster Anthony Spilotro threatens to erupt into a mob war.

"I know of no basis for that story," Rosenthal told the SUN in an interview. "I think the story is totally erroneous. I would not be surprised if it's some kind of a ploy that law enforcement has decided to use to further their best interests rather than being objective or totally honest.

"I would be very interested to know the origin of the story. Obviously, I do not have that luxury."

The SUN quoted law enforcement sources Tuesday as ... between Rosenthal and Spilotro, both alleged

The story said the rift between Rosenthal and Spilotro was sparked by a Sept. 8 argument between Rosenthal and his wife, Geri, who reportedly admitted having a relationship with Spilotro.

During the argument at the couple's Las Vegas Country Club home, Geri allegedly pointed a gun at Rosenthal and was disarmed by Spilotro's wife, Nancy, as a dozen neighbors and police watched.

Rosenthal, who said he had spoken to his wife by telephone Friday, insisted that she was misquoted by law enforcement sources in the SUN story.

"I spoke to my wife this morning, and I know that law enforcement would be very disappointed that Geri Rosenthal is not in any position to cooperate with them.

"Law enforcement was very hopeful that if they were to ... Geri Rosenthal by breaking the law, that maybe they ...

Rosenthal refused to discuss specifics of the reported rift between him and Spilotro other than to deny the allegations and say both men were still friends. He declined to say whether he had spoken with Spilotro since Sept. 8

A former Stardust entertainment director under Allen R. Glick's Argent Corp., Rosenthal also refused to be pinned down on whether he has replaced Oscar Goodman as his attorney.

Goodman has represented both Rosenthal and Spilotro in the past. But Rosenthal's divorce proceedings and federal lawsuit against Metro Police are being handled by attorney Eric Zubel.

Rosenthal, who said he is "comfortable" with Zubel, filed a federal lawsuit seeking up to $6 million in damages against police Thursday, charging they helped his wife steal some $1.2 million in jewelry and cash from safe deposit boxes following ...

Rosenthal said he was convinced Metro Police ly broke the law by escorting his wife to the ba... her take the jewelry and then preventing Rose... stopping her flight to California.

"I think they were grasping for an opportun... aside the law because it was Frank Rosenthal...

"It appears to me that they decided, by thei... the law wasn't very important and that it wou... best interests to break the law to further their ob... upon me and my family and possibly others. ... break the law, I'll eat your newspaper. We're ... them held accountable for what they did."

Rosenthal said he and his wife intend ... differences without fanfare.

"My wife and I are going to make every a... things out . . . in a dignified manner without ... We both feel confident that we can do this ...

The Saga in Black and White

Part of what made the Argent Corporation drama so compelling was it played out in headlines, with players such as Frank Rosenthal's then-attorney, Oscar Goodman, remaining a part of the Las Vegas political scene today. In the 1950s and 1960s, the mob's behind-the-scenes influence was the town's worst-kept secret. Even in the 1970s Argent case, the word "mob" doesn't often show up in print until it appears the government is winning.

A sampling of local news stories as the saga unfolded:

Frank Rosenthal named consultant at LV Hotels

Argent Corporation has announced the appointment of casino executive Frank Rosenthal to the office of executive consultant to the chairman of the board.

Allen R. Glick, president and chairman of the board of Argent, said Rosenthal would serve as the corporation's executive consultant for the Stardust and Fremont Hotels.

Rosenthal, 45, a native of Chicago, has been prominent in the Las Vegas gaming industry for the past 10 years. He resides here with his wife Geri; son, Steve, 4, and daughter, Stephanie, 1.

The vital, new post being filled by Rosenthal will see him conferring with and recommending to Glick, "policies which will insure the integrity and standards of the resort-gaming industry and Argent Corporation."
— *Argent Corporation press release printed in local newspapers; October 22, 1974*

Dateline: Las Vegas

Frank "Lefty" Rosenthal, suddenly and almost magically, has become one of the most important gambling executives in Nevada.

But it is interesting that the rank-and-file of the industry . . . are asking, "Who the hell is Rosenthal and where did he come from?" You would think he was some sort of mystery man.

Well, he's no mystery man. Those of us who have known him for years, some much longer than me, acknowledge that he is one of the smartest — and he may be THE smartest — professional gambler, pricemaker and former bookmaker in the game.
— *Paul Price column,* Las Vegas Sun*; January 15, 1975*

Will Rosenthal be licensed?

After many months of mental gymnastics, the Gaming Commission will finally enter the ring next month to render the long-awaited decision on licensing Frank Rosenthal as an executive of Argent Corp.

There is talk that there will be allegations of association with hoodlums hurled against Rosenthal. Such charges, however, are usually based on heresay and the applicant and his superb legal counsel shouldn't have any trouble disposing of such claims.
— *Dick Odessky column,* Valley Times*; December 10, 1975*

Lefty Gets 'Thumbs Down'

CARSON CITY (UPI) — The State Gaming Control Board Yesterday recommended denial of a Nevada gaming license for professional gambler Frank Rosenthal on grounds he was involved in two bribery attempts of college athletes in

1960.

Rosenthal sought to be director of Nevada operations for the Argent Corporation, which runs the Stardust and Fremont Hotel-Casinos in Las Vegas. The vote by the three-member board was unanimous.

Board member Jack Stratton said the state "cannot risk fixing the stamp of approval on Mr. Rosenthal." He said the licensing of Rosenthal would reflect discredit on the state and the gaming industry.

— Las Vegas Sun; *January 16, 1976*

Rosenthal returns to Argent as food and beverage director

Frank Rosenthal went to work Monday morning as food and beverage director of Argent Corp. — not the executive gaming post he filled only last week, but one in which he said he can make a sub-

stantial contribution.

Rosenthal was forced to give up his key executive post with Argent . . . when the Nevaada Supreme Court upheld the action of the Gaming Commission last year in denying him a license.

— Las Vegas Review-Journal; *February 7, 1977*

Rosenthal denies 'war' with Spilotro near

Ex-gaming figure Frank Rosenthal Friday denied allegations in the Sun that a rift between the former Stardust Hotel executive and reputed mobster Anthony Spilotro threatens to erupt into a mob war.

The Sun quoted law enforcement sources Tuesday as saying the rift between Rosenthal and Spilotro, both alleged watchdogs for the Chicago Crime syndicate's Las Vegas interests, could develop into a mob war involving reputed Chicago crime boss Joseph Aiuppa.

The story said the rift between Rosenthal and Spilotro was sparked by a Sept. 8 arguemant between Rosenthal and his wife Geri, who reportedly admitted having a relationshop with Spilotro.

During the argument at the couple's Las Vegas Country Club home, Geri allegedly pointed a gun at Rosenthal and was disarmed by Spilotro's wife, Nancy, as a dozen neighbors and police watched.

— Las Vegas Sun; *October 11, 1980*

Police probe Rosenthal car blast

Las Vegas police inspectors were expected to interview reputed organized crime figure Frank "Lefty" Rosenthal today in efforts to find out who tried to kill him Monday night by bombing his car.

The well-known football handicapper survived a bomb explosion when the blast threw him

through an open door, authorities said.

— Las Vegas Review-Journal, *October 5, 1982*

FBI: Chicago mob put 'hit' on Rosenthal

There is "no question" the attempt on Frank "Lefty" Rosenthal's life Monday night was the result of a mob contract originating from Chicago, the FBI said Wednesday.

Charlie Parsons, the bureau's agent in charge of the organized-crime division, talked to Rosenthal "for several hours" Wednesday. "We haven't identified the guy who placed the bomb in his car, but there's no question in our minds it came from Chicago. It was a mob contract."

The Review-Journal learned law enforcement circles seriously suspect the personal feud between Rosenthal and Anthony "Tony the Ant" Spilotro played a part.

Spilotro is considered the Chicago mob's overseer in Las Vegas, who controls the street rackets and gets a percentage of all the illegal bookmaking in Las Vegas, according to IRS affidavits.

Rosenthal at one time had been the No. 2 man at Allen Glick's Argent Corp., which owned the Stardust . . . But Glick was forced by Nevada gaming officials to sell out in 1979, following an investigation of a multimillion-dollar slot skimming operation tied to the Chicago mob.

— Las Vegas Review-Journal, *October 7, 1982*

Rosenthal says feds think Spilotro did it

Asked if he agreed Spilotro of the Chicago mob were behind the bombing, Rosenthal said, "I know it didn't come from the Boy Scouts of America."

— Valley Times; *October 7, 1982*

Shirley Brancucci: The Baccarat Shoe Crosses Gender Lines

"Around here it was always a party," says Shirley Brancucci, who started at the Stardust as a cocktail waitress and eventually became a baccarat pit boss.

Brancucci came to Las Vegas from Newport, Kentucky In 1952. "There was bad talk about waitresses years ago," she said. "They say all that stuff about the bosses making you do this or that. That wasn't true." Undaunted, she felt it presented a good opportunity for her and her two children. "I felt there was more money here."

She started as a cocktail waitress but eventually became the first female baccarat dealer on the Strip. That honor earned her a spot on Alan King's TV show ("I had my 15 minutes of fame") as well as Frank Rosenthal's local TV show that first aired in 1977.

"He made me (go on it)," she said of the broadcast helmed by the limelight-loving Rosenthal as "entertainment director" of the property. "It was the worst show in town."

THE FRANK ROSENTHAL SHOW

FRANK ROSENTHAL, LEFT, CHATS WITH FRANK...
...Sinatra's plea for UNLV Rebels goes unh...

One of Frank Rosenthal's most quirky conceits was hosting a TV show from the Stardust. Guests included Robert Conrad, opposite top, Jill St. John, bottom, and the big coup, Frank Sinatra. Alas, that particular show went unseen due to a technical malfunction.

bookmaking business didn't allow for that.

"Normal" proved relative in early 1971, when Rosenthal — as manager of the Rose Bowl Sports Book — was one of five men indicted on federal charges of illegally using telephones for interstate betting (the case was dismissed in 1975 when a federal judge ruled wiretap evidence

Sinatra raps NCAA in show that didn't air

Pg. 3   Aug. 29, 1977

The return of "The Frank Rosenthal Show" was spoiled Saturday night when a tape machine at KSHO-TV, Channel 13, apparently broke down and technicians at the station were unable to fix it or run the back-up tape.

The show, which had been heavily advertised all week long, was billed as the first show ever to be aired live from a Las Vegas casino, the Stardust. It was to be shown in 49 cities in 29 states.

KSHO officials could not be contacted for comment Monday morning.

The first show starred Frank Sinatra, Jill St. John, Robert Conrad and various members of the television show "Baa Baa Black Sheep."

Persons who saw the show while it was taped said the highlight was an impromptu plea from Sinatra to Las Vegans to fight the NCAA two-year probation of UNLV. Sinatra was reported to have said there undoubtedly were some infractions, but a two-year penalty is too stiff.

He told Vegans to sign petitions backing the basketball program and send them to the NCAA.

The show was sponsored by the Stardust. Officials there said the show was one of the best to come out of Las Vegas, and its publicity value would have been enormous.

A meeting is scheduled with KSHO-TV to discuss the breakdown and the station's performance Saturday night. Stardust officials and the show's producers reportedly were meeting with lawyers to discuss the result of the show not being aired on a syndicated basis across the nation when it should have been.

When the Rosenthal show tape was gobbled by the machine, reportedly no technicians were on duty to fix the machine or run the back-up tape. Consequently, viewers saw and heard only the opening of the show, a whirl and blur, then a still picture of a little man, half way up a telephone pole saying, "One Moment Please."

The sign stayed on the air for about an hour.

inadmissable).

But Rosenthal was impressed by the easy flow of money he saw in the casino, and realized that he could do much to increase that flow. This would be way easier than running a bookie operation. When Glick's Argent company took over, one of the first things his backers told him to do was promote Rosenthal.

Rosenthal's rapid rise from floor supervisor caught the attention of gaming officials and prompted his long struggle to be licensed as a key employee. Rosenthal's legacy includes the 1975 introduction of the outsized race and sports book with multiple TV screens and individual betting cubicles, now a vital part of any casino operation. But in the beginning, he and Glick butted heads repeatedly. It wasn't long before Chicago let the young developer know who really was in charge.

The employees knew, too.

"Glick was a cover for Rosenthal," Warden said.

And while she, Brancucci and longtime cocktail server Carol Geraci all express affection for Al Sachs and Herb Tobman, general managers during that era, they weren't as fond of Lefty.

"He was a disgusting man," Warden said.

Brancucci minces her words a little more, but she wasn't much of a fan either. After working at the Desert Inn, Sands, Riviera and Tropicana,

An early 1990s renovation iof the main casino ncluded the colorful poolside Terrace Bar, right. Below, the Stardust played up its "legendary" status with souvenir drink glasses during its final year of operation. Opposite, a 1980s guest directory included this floor plan of the resort.

she'd been serving cocktails at the Stardust since 1969, and by 1972 decided it was time to move on. "I went to dealer school because I felt I was too old for cocktails," Brancucci said.

Sachs told her he was going to put her in the baccarat pit. With Rosenthal.

"He'll kill me!" Brancucci told Sachs.

She continuously tangled with Rosenthal. He would scream at her, but knew she was a skilled dealer. "It was a love-hate relationship," she said.

Then came one Thanksgiving day. Brancucci was so sick she couldn't go to work. She called in, but so had a group of fellow

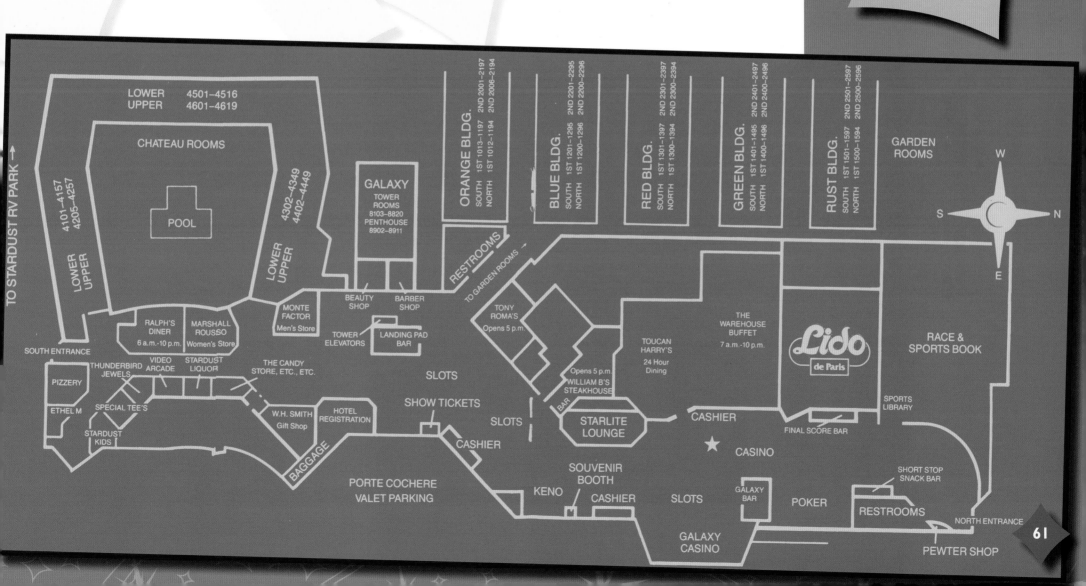

TO STARDUST RV PARK →

LOWER 4501–4516
UPPER 4601–4619

CHATEAU ROOMS

4302–4349
4402–4449

LOWER
UPPER

4101–4157
4205–4257

LOWER
UPPER

POOL

GALAXY
TOWER
ROOMS
8103–8820
PENTHOUSE
8902–8911

ORANGE BLDG.
SOUTH 1ST 1013–1197 2ND 2001–2197
NORTH 1ST 1012–1194 2ND 2006–2194

BLUE BLDG.
SOUTH 1ST 1201–1295 2ND 2201–2295
NORTH 1ST 1200–1296 2ND 2200–2296

RED BLDG.
SOUTH 1ST 1301–1397 2ND 2301–2397
NORTH 1ST 1300–1394 2ND 2300–2394

GREEN BLDG.
SOUTH 1ST 1401–1495 2ND 2401–2497
NORTH 1ST 1400–1496 2ND 2400–2496

RUST BLDG.
SOUTH 1ST 1501–1597 2ND 2501–2597
NORTH 1ST 1500–1594 2ND 2500–2596

GARDEN
ROOMS

W
S — N
E

RESTROOMS

TO GARDEN ROOMS →

BEAUTY
SHOP

BARBER
SHOP

MONTE
FACTOR
Men's Store

TOWER
ELEVATORS

LANDING PAD
BAR

TONY
ROMA'S
Opens 5 p.m.

TOUCAN
HARRY'S
24 Hour
Dining

THE
WAREHOUSE
BUFFET
7 a.m.–10 p.m.

Lido
de Paris

RACE &
SPORTS BOOK

RALPH'S
DINER
6 a.m.–10 p.m.

MARSHALL
ROUSSO
Women's Store

SOUTH ENTRANCE

THUNDERBIRD
JEWELS

VIDEO
ARCADE

STARDUST
LIQUOR

THE CANDY
STORE, ETC., ETC.

SLOTS

PIZZERY

ETHEL M

SPECIAL TEE'S

STARDUST
KIDS

W.H. SMITH
Gift Shop

HOTEL
REGISTRATION

SHOW TICKETS

Opens 5 p.m.
WILLIAM B'S
STEAKHOUSE

BAR

SPORTS
LIBRARY

FINAL SCORE BAR

CASHIER

SLOTS

STARLITE
LOUNGE

CASHIER

BAGGAGE

CASHIER

PORTE COCHERE
VALET PARKING

KENO

SOUVENIR
BOOTH

CASHIER

SLOTS

GALAXY
BAR

POKER

★ CASINO

SHORT STOP
SNACK BAR

RESTROOMS

NORTH ENTRANCE

GALAXY
CASINO

PEWTER SHOP

Siegfried & Roy: Lefty Works Magic

The *Casino* movie depicted it as a joke when Robert De Niro's "Lefty" Rosenthal character, denied a gaming license as a key employee, had to pretend to be the casino's entertainment director.

But German illusionists Siegfried & Roy made the jump from unbilled specialty act to top-billed stars of *Lido de Paris* under Rosenthal's watch at the Stardust, lending credence to the notion that maybe Lefty earned the entertainment director title after all. Awash in his odd niche of fame after the movie came out, Rosenthal detailed his version of how the deal went down in a 1998 column for a publication called *Insider Viewpoint of Las Vegas*.

Rosenthal claimed that when he learned Siegfried & Roy were facing a renewal of their contract in a rival pro-

duction at the MGM Grand Hotel, he made a pitch to "an ambitious young man named Bernie Yuman, a bearded gofer . . . a hang-around fixture of sorts. He seemed eager to accept any challenge within reasonable limits." So Rosenthal offered Yuman $500 if he could deliver the two magicians to his office for a meeting.

"Bernie was excited. He had 20 minutes before the finale of the second show at the MGM and hit the front door of the Stardust at a dead run," Rosenthal wrote.

Yuman offers his own account in Annette Tapert's authorized biography *Siegfried & Roy: Mastering the Impossible*. Oddly enough, he makes no mention of the $500, just as Rosenthal's

version makes no mention of Yuman's claim that the MGM's revue had put a big dent in *Lido*. "They weren't doing more than 600 people a show and 300 for the third show on Saturday night. By the time they came to me, they had canceled that third performance," Yuman recalled.

The two stories do match up in terms of Yuman crashing the dressing room of Siegfried & Roy — whom he had never met — and sweet-talking them into a meeting the next day. A day after that, "We signed a deal with the Stardust that was historic in every way," Yuman claimed. "For the first time ever, an act would have 33 minutes onstage, which was really a show within a show. They received 100 percent star billing equal to the title of the show."

And from that day forward, Yuman was

the duo's manager. Rosenthal said fancy dressing rooms and special arrangements for the duo's animals was the easy part. The star billing was the toughest thing to work out with *Lido* officials. He called the coup "the steal of the decade, probably second only to the Brinks armored car robbery." Rival hotels were "asleep at the switch and by the time they woke up, the best show on earth was out of their casino and down the street."

Siegfried & Roy joined *Lido* in July 1978 and stayed until 1981, when circus promoters Irvin and Kenneth Feld financed *Beyond Belief* at the Frontier Hotel.

In September 1975, the Stardust had a new calling card: a $100,000 betting limit — on a Strip where the standard cap ranged from $1,000 to $5,000. "If you've got the money and courage, then we've got the place for you to wager," hotel president Burton Brown proclaimed.

dealers who were going skiing. Lefty punished them all by putting them on day shift.

"Day shift was awful for me," Brancucci said. Although it didn't affect her economically because dealers split their tips, it did impinge on the time she could spend with her kids. "Dancing and Brownies and Girl Scouts. I called my mother and had her come out." And then a few weeks later, she was among a group of friends (and friends of friends) who were having a few drinks at the Tropicana. They got to talking about their jobs , and she lamented the problems with her shift. The next day, she went to work and Rosenthal told her curtly that she was back on swing shift.

"Your friend Tony called me," he said.

Tony? Who was Tony? She couldn't think of any friend named Tony who would hold much sway with Rosenthal. So she put in a call to one of the friends with whom

she'd been drinking at the Tropicana.

Oh, she was told, that would be Tony Spilotro. A friend and associate of Rosenthal since his days in Chicago, Spilotro was known to be an enforcer for the mob there. "He was a scary guy," Brancucci said of Rosenthal. "But I stood up to him. I didn't know how not to. There's been a lot of times it caused me a lot of problems."

But for the most part, the employees and former employees said they weren't all that concerned about the mob ownership and the skimming operation that funneled millions in cash from the count room back to mobsters in Chicago, Kansas City, Milwaukee and Cleveland.

"It's a sense of excitement," Warden said. "I thought I was protected. I was good for the place. The people who did the skimming weren't going to hurt me because I brought people to the tables."

Len Rader, who went to work as a light man at the Stardust in 1958, said he was oblivious to the mob ownership connections for the most part.

He does remember when stage manager Bill DeAngelis asked him and a sound man to take a visitor around town.

"After he left, we were told he was a lieutenant," Rader said.

"Once in a while we heard about somebody who'd been picked up in the desert with broken knees or something, but they didn't bother us," he said.

"We were very small potatoes," Jill Rader said.

"We knew them all – but in a nice way," Brancucci said.

"They were good to people," Seely said. "They knew if you made money, they made money."

Below, a topping-off ceremony that included Bill Boyd, center left, and Sam Boyd, center right, and the requisite showgirls, celebrated the arrival of 32-story tower on November 9, 1991.

Plush Chairs, TVs and More Money!

If Frank Rosenthal hadn't been overseeing casinos that, in the words of one news account, "were operating the largest skim ever uncovered in Nevada," he might be hailed as a visionary. His lasting contribution was bringing the race and sports book out of seedy shopping centers near the Strip and turning them into vital revenue generators for corporate Las Vegas.

The Stardust's 8,000 square-foot race and sports book opened in September 1975, ushering in the modern era of a multiple TV screens — well, at least three, to cover all the networks — and plush chairs.

The sports book was perfectly timed with the expansion of sports coverage on TV. *The Stardust Line* became the early word on point spreads as well as a long-running radio show broadcast on KWDN-AM 720. Until closing day, the sports book held onto its own unique charm, thanks to the loyal "characters" who populated it.

The Stardust Sports Book as seen when it opened in 1975, above, and in its final summer of operation, left, in 2006. Right and opposite page: Football great Jim Brown and Lee Pete hosted The Stardust Line, *which gamblers tuned to from 1981 to 2006.*

THE STARDUST LINE
WITH
LEE PETE
JIM BROWN

BROADCAST LIVE
FROM THE
STARDUST RACE &
SPORTSBOOK

SATURDAY & SUNDAY NIGHTS
10 P.M. - MIDNITE
KDWN RADIO

FEATURING MANY GUESTS FROM
THE SPORTSWORLD

You are invited to attend
FREE

Sam Boyd leads the first tour of the Olde-Tyme Gambling Museum, which opened at the Stardust in 1987.

Lefty Leaves The Picture

But by 1983, the FBI and state gaming regulators had finally triumphed in the long *Casino* drama, events of which included Spilotro's arrest for heading a burglary ring, the 1982 bombing of Rosenthal's car in the restaurant parking lot, and the Los Angeles death of Rosenthal's wife Geri — who had an affair with Spilotro — of a mysterious drug overdose later that year. The state suspended, pending revocation, the gaming license of the Argent principals. Rosenthal moved to California after attaining the rare honor of being listed in the "Black Book," the state Gaming Commission list of "excluded persons" not allowed to enter casinos.

The final chapter would play out three years later, when Spilotro and his brother were found beaten to death and buried in a shallow grave in an Indiana cornfield, presumably in retaliation for the recklessness that helped the government build its case and send six mob bosses to prison.

The state asked Boyd Gaming to manage the property. At the time, Boyd Gaming owned the California and Sam's Town, and the family owned the Eldorado and Joker's Wild.

"I was maybe somewhat naive," Bill Boyd says today. A number of friends called him. "Have you lost all your marbles?" he remembers as the gist of the conversations. "These people you're dealing with … You should be very concerned."

And indeed, "it was very adversarial at first," Boyd said. Argent retained management of the non-gaming areas of the property, and at first didn't cooperate when it came to getting hotel rooms for casino guests. Eventually, Boyd said, they realized that cooperation would only make them money.

Boyd's company was hired for a flat fee, "which was very minimal," and the profits went to the licensee. (After it was all over, Boyd said, he was asked by the state what he'd change about the process. He suggested that, in such cases, the casino profits be held in escrow, and not given to the licensee if the license is revoked. The change ultimately was implemented.)

Brancucci remembers the beginning of the end.

"It was in December '83, right before Christmas," she said. "I was in the baccarat pit when the federal agents came in.

"And they fired just about everybody. Almost all the floor people were fired. And management."

Geraci remembers talking to one manager who thought he'd survive the changeover.

"He was fired the next morning," she said.

"It was tense when the Boyds came in,"

Brancucci said. "Especially for me. I thought I was going to get fired."

Boyd said that after about a year of his company managing the Stardust casino, an Argent attorney reported that he thought Argent would lose its appeal, and asked if Boyd Gaming was interested in buying the Stardust and the Fremont. Ownership officially changed on February 28, 1985.

"We've worked diligently to keep it on par," Boyd said. The company spent $50 million

Boyd Gaming took over management of the Stardust in 1983. The company passed from the hands of founder Sam Boyd, right, to his son, Bill, upon the elder Boyd's death in 1993.

The Stardust left the high rollers to the Sands and Desert Inn, embracing the middle-market gamblers drawn to its expansive 16,500-square-foot casino.

to expand and overhaul the property in 1988, then added the 32-story hotel tower in 1991, "which were very modern rooms at the time."

The company went public in 1993. It now is the third-largest gaming company in the world.

"It's changed a lot," Brancucci said. "How do you explain corporations from the mob?"

Of Las Vegas in general, Jill Rader said, "It's all these young men with these degrees in business administration. It's not fun. We were lucky to work in Las Vegas when it was fun."

Three eras of hotel history: This vantage point from the Stardust grounds in its final summer shows a room wing from the old Royal Nevada at bottom right. Behind that is the nine-story Galaxy Tower, added in 1964. And the big purple building behind that is the 32-story tower that opened in 1991.

Dreaming of a Song

A French import gives Las Vegas a new look

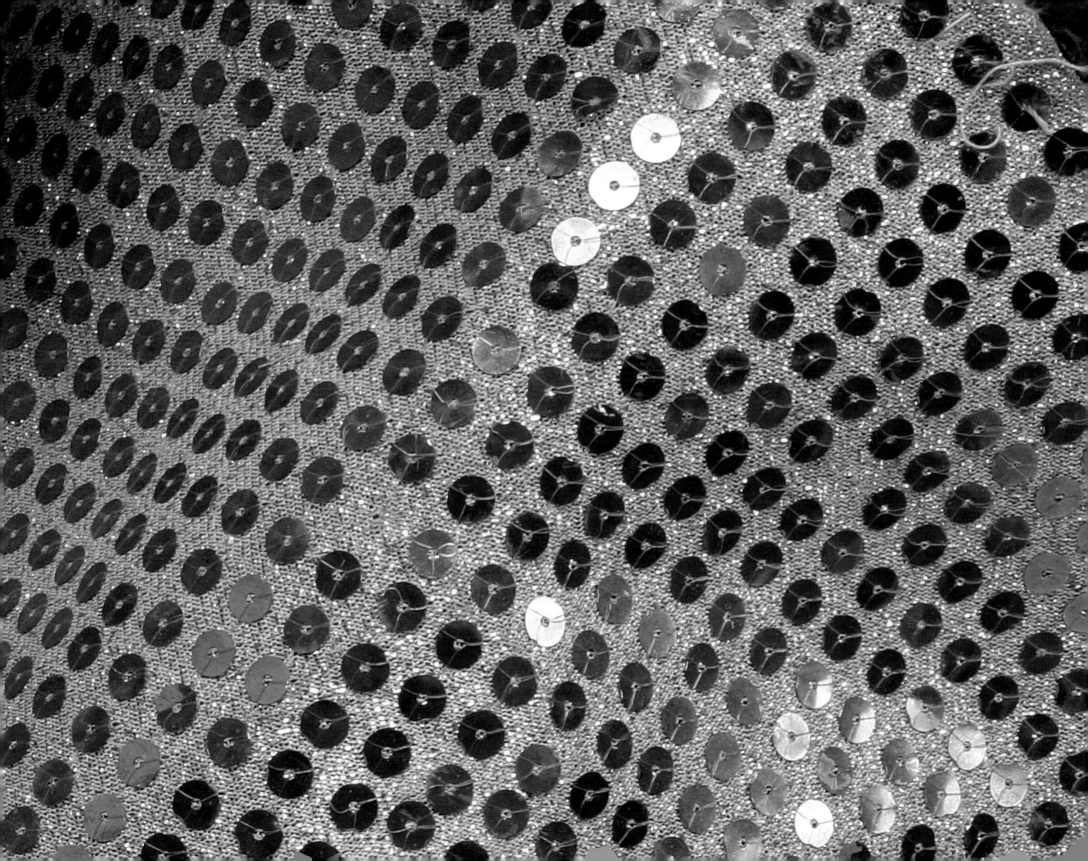

AMERICA'S MOST SPECTACULAR HOTEL presents THE CONTINENT'S MOST LAVISH AND EXCITING SHOW!

STARDUST LAS VEGAS

78

Direct from Paris

Through all the changes and turnover that surrounded the Stardust construction, one big idea managed to come to port. A really big idea.

Lido de Paris became synonymous with the casino, and eventually helped Las Vegas steal the Parisian image of the showgirl in high heels and feathery headpiece as its own icon.

STARDUST

Styled in breath-taking splendor elegance, America's most spectac new 700-seat theatre-restaurant, bri the Continental Touch to Las Vegas! Here will thrill to lavish productions featuring stars of Hollywood, Broadway, Paris, the Wo Here, too, you will delight in cuisine prepared world-renowned chefs and served in the classic Con ental tradition.

The must-see import drew the high rollers and national attention, more than compensating for the Stardust's middlebrow approach to architecture and room volume.

"We didn't have large retail complexes, a litany of restaurants," said Bill Boyd, chairman and CEO of Boyd Gaming Corporation, who first visited the property long before his company owned it. "Entertainment was one of the ways you attracted visitors to Las Vegas."

The Stardust was four years in construction before it came under the control of Desert Inn operator Moe Dalitz. Frank Sennes, the Desert Inn's entertainment director, used choreographer Donn Arden's chorus girls at that hotel and his Moulin Rouge nightclub in Hollywood. He knew Arden also went back and forth to France as the choreographer of *Lido*, a Paris cabaret revue since 1946.

When Dalitz was put in charge of the Stardust, Sennes "went to New York to look for some acts," he recalled in 1991. "I called Moe Dalitz and said, `I'm going to Paris to see

Opposite page: Program cover from the fourth edition of Lido. *Right, a newspaper ad touts the arrival of "the gayest of gay shows" in 1958.*

The original Lido showgirls arrive to a reception of French champagne and American hot dogs. The airport publicity photo would be repeated in different variations for each new cast.

ON STAGE!

in the *Cafe Continental*

Styled in breath-taking splendor and elegance, America's most spectacular new 700-seat theater-restaurant brings the Continental Touch to Las Vegas! Here you will thrill to lavish productions featuring the stars of Hollywood...Broadway...the world! Here, too, you will delight in cuisine prepared by world-renown chefs and served in the classic Continental tradition.

★ A history-making entertainment event...the first show ever brought <u>intact</u> from Europe to Las Vegas! ★ The gayest of gay sho from the most exciting city in the world...direct from the internationally-acclaimed Lido Club on the Champs-Elysées, Paris...

LE LIDO DE PARIS
"C'est Magnifique"

Conceived by Pierre-Louis Guerin & Rene Fraday
Staged by Donn Arden

FEATURING
The darling of Paris

JACQUELINE DU BIEF

The World-Famed Bluebell Girls

plus Mammoth On-Stage Aquacade!
★ Exciting Ice Show! ★ Neapolitan Street Scene!
★ Spicy Mademoiselles! Promenade of European Beauties!
★ Giant Fireworks Display from Eiffel Tower!
★ Astonishing Multi-Stages!

STARDUST

WORLD'S LARGEST RESORT HOTE

OVER 1,000 ROOMS PRICED FROM $6!
Luxurious guest accommodations, each with "at-door" parking, have been designed and furnished with impeccable taste! Each room has individually controlled air-conditioning. You live like a millionaire at low cost.

SUPERLATIVE FOOD AT MODERATE PRICES!
Dine in a setting to match your mood! In the Palm Room, at the Pool Pavilion, or in the Cafe Continental you will delight in delicacies from the four corners of the world, prepared by master chefs.

A WORLD OF FUN AWAI
Enjoy entertainment unlimited, twenty Stellar attractions at the Bar and in the ... Largest swimming pool in Las Vegas... fun for which Las Vegas is famous is you the largest, most exciting resort hotel h

what's going on over there.'" When he saw the *Lido de Paris*, he knew "there were no big shows like it in Las Vegas."

Sennes and Arden worked with *Lido* director Pierre Louis-Guerin to bring the show to Las Vegas. To get ready for it on the homefront, the showroom, Cafe Continental, was fitted with six hydraulic stages that could be raised and lowered separately or locked together, an 11-by-30-foot swimming pool and an ice rink that could be brought to stage level in 15 seconds.

Ooh La La!

The show debuted on the hotel's opening day, July 2, 1958, before an audience of 700 that included Bob Hope, Harold Lloyd and the McGuire Sisters. The skaters and hydraulics were impressive, but what really got them talking was something that was missing entirely on many of the girls: Brassieres.

Las Vegas had leaned heavily toward cheescake imagery all throughout its rapid expansion in the 1950s. Most of the star revues at the Sands included a line of chorus girls as a warm-up act for the featured star. Smaller casinos that couldn't afford big names found it convenient that television was killing burlesque houses in the big cities; the dancers were welcome here. But it was still more "tease" than "strip." The dancers wore pasties on their breasts until January 1957, when *Minsky's*

Though modest by the standards of today's automated stagecraft, the original Lido *marked the first use of hydraulic lifts and an ice rink on a Las Vegas stage.*

The waterfall was a dramatic scenic effect that enabled producers to create various disasters onstage, such as a mythical breaking of Hoover Dam for "The Valley in Peril" in the fourth edition and "The Punishment of the Gods" in the 1978 African tableau.

Follies opened at the Dunes.

That paved the way for *Lido* to be presented just as it was in Paris. And it did not go unnoticed. As Les Devor wrote in the *Las Vegas Review-Journal*, "From the ceiling descend platforms, each with a bare-bosomed beauty, standing cool as you please, and before the surprise has caused nearsighted gentlemen to repair their thoughtlessness by putting on glasses, the girls are whisked upward into the rafters."

The revue even drew the attention of *Life* magazine in the Christmas issue of 1958: "The *Lido* girls got to Las Vegas in time for a great public argument over whether bosoms should be covered or not. To them, this seemed silly. 'It's ridiculous,' said Sheila Shephard of England. 'If people don't want to see undraped bodies, they should go where bodies are draped'."

That the show was European — and therefore inarguably sophisticated — kept long-running controversy to a minimum.

"It was so beautiful. You were never really conscious of the girls being nude. It was always done with dignity," original cast member Valda Esau recalled years later.

"*Lido* was the show to see," said Larry Seely, who started work as a Stardust bellman just two months after the hotel-casino opened.

Seely remembers that in those days, rooms cost only $6 a night. And, since a room guaranteed that one could buy tickets for the show, "Some people got a room and never even stayed in it." He also remembers people paying the bellmen to get them the best possible tickets: "The amount of the tip decided where you were going to go (in the showroom)."

Len Rader began work as a light operator at

Vegas Daze and Nites

By Ralph Pearl

STARDUST FOLLIES: — It's so vast. It's so electrifying. It's spectacular. And, of course, I'm reffering to the Paris Lido show which came to life a couple of nights ago in the Continental Cafe of the Stardust Hotel. The many tastily attired and unattired young ladies and gents add an eye appealing flavor to the "C'est Magnifique" revue while many of the European acts add the zest and talent.

Like, for instance, let's take Marvyn Rody, a sleight of hander who stuns the first nighters with his magical carrying on. A great favorite in the Parisian music halls, Marvyn tops off his routine by exhaling hundreds of tiny, lit electric light bulbs strung together in a clothes line effect. And don't ask how the bulbs got there in the first place. For Martha Raye it might have been easy and understandable. Suffice to say, it was quite a stunt.

Now the stage came alive. A lot of naked chests, attached to pretty gals, came down on elevators from the ceiling! Other naked chests, attached to other pretty girls, made up the backdrop. They came up from sunken stages and off the wings. In a couple of minutes a curtain went up revealing a huge swimming pool and some more naked mermaids.

Shades of Cecil B. DeMille! What next? Well, no sooner said than done. The swimming pool disappeared promptly in front of the naked eye and was replaced by an ice skating rink and the delightful skating Jacqueline Du Bief.

Add an energetic juggler of crockery, Eric Brenn, la favorite doll, Reuby Bruce, and the hit act of the whole show, comics Georges Campo and zany Lina Marvell who cavort-ing and caper about in skill-

of Fox Movietone News on Pacific Coast) celebrated their 24th anny . . . The California Club's Phil Long is installing a nickel slot machine with all proceeds to City of Hope . . . New Frontier licensee matter up for final consideration last week in July. If the green light is given Jack Barenfeld and company, look for an August 1 opening . . . Jimmy Stewart and Sam Ledner (stage manager) have left the Tropicana.

Lonesome George Gobel drops in Sunday evening at 6:15 to chat with your's truly on the "Ralph Pearl Celebrity Corner" Channel 8. The man with the buzz saw haircut will reveal how he became a top TV favorite over night after many years in the saloon circuit. The Riviera star is packing them them into the Clover room always.

An absolute must: The rib tickling mimicries of Carol Burnett in the Ed Sullivan show at the Desert Inn . . . Eddie Fisher stays at Tropicana until August 5, seven weeks in all. Carol Channing follows Eddie.

RALPH PEARL SHOW, SUNDAY 6:15, CHANNEL 8. GUEST: GEORGE GOBEL

Wears Lu

Myron
luck char
blue shirt
used to
Wisconsin
donned
"27 Wa

He
theatre
his st
for Se
ing
form.

Again on the filming of "Sergeants Warner Bros., McCormick arrived at the studio attired in the blue shirt.

'Playbill' At Brussels

NEW YORK (AP) — Broadway's own program, "Playbill," is appearing in a special overseas edition at the Brussels World's Fair.

"Playbill," which is used in all the White Way's legitimate theaters, is being printed abroad in English, French and Flemish.

Now the stage came alive. A lot of naked chests, attached to pretty gals, came down on elevators from the ceiling! Other naked chests, attached to other pretty girls, made up the backdrop. They came up from sunken stages and off the wings. In a couple of minutes a curtain went up revealing a huge swimming pool and some more naked mermaids.

Initial reactions to Lido de Paris as reflected by columnists for the Las Vegas Sun, above, and Las Vegas Review-Journal, opposite page. Both opted for humorous spins on the groundbreaking use of topless showgirls. Bare breasts had previously been displayed only in a Harold Minsky burlesque revue at the Dunes.

Magnificent Stardust Opens Smash Show

Las Vegas REVIEW-JOURNAL

Entertainment Section

VOL. L. NO. 181   LAS VEGAS, NEVADA, FRIDAY, JULY 4, 1958   10c PER COPY   28 PAGES

PINKY PACKS 'EM IN — Pinky Lee continues to draw SRO crowds in the Dunes Hotel Minsky's. His original six he is starred in "Life Begins to 15, an all-time Las Vegas "Step" hotel revue "Lees" Diamond, The Marquis Family and beautiful Minsky girls. Three shows nightly

Vegas Vagaries

By LES DEVOR

There is something akin to an air of expectancy when a new resort hotel opens its doors to the public. The crowds of curious and well-wishers mill onto the new carpets, grind out cigarettes, and thus another ten million dollar hotel is launched. And so the Stardust was launched.

The excitement of the moment is caught up with the stream of people and the hour everyone waited for has arrived.

Thus the Stardust was born for the nation's press Wednesday night when the key to the Stardust was thrown away, and the strip's largest hotel hosted its first guests.

Those who were fortunate enough to receive bids to the press premiere cued up before the entrance to the Continental Cafe where the seating was being carried out with dispatch, as snatches of conversation drifted about. Comparisons were natural, and retrospectively, the Stardust comes out ahead of many first-night openers, both from the time it took to seat its first 700 guests and then to serve them.

There is so much to report about the hotel, the show, and the opening itself. From the moment George Jessel stepped through the curtains with his opening greetings, until he reappeared at the close of the most spectacular presentation ever seen here, some hour and forty-five minutes later, those attending the premiere were treated to a truly Continental flavor. And a goodly number in the audience appreciated the exciting tang of La Belle France and its famous Lido show, since they comprise a segment of the international set and have seen the Lido show in its original setting.

Those who have seen the show in Paris say it has lost none of the flavor, nor any of the zest of its Parisian counterpart, as it was brought here intact from Europe.

... of the show is enhanced

... things are bigger and better at the Stardust.

The show, "C'est Magnifique," had its unveiling before a host of celebrities, columnists, and feature writers, as well as many distinguished members of the state's political and economic community, all of whom welcomed the newcomer to the entertainment capital of the world, some with congratulatory "play," and others with sincere well-wishes.

The moment has come to deal with the show itself, and the first thought that rushes to perceptive is the words to a song of many years ago that went something like . . . "How you gonna keep them down on the farm after they've seen Paree? . . ."

House lights dim, there's a few bars of overture, and from the ceiling of the Continental Cafe descend platforms, each with a bare-bosomed beauty, standing cool as you please, and before the surprise has caused nearsighted gentlemen to repair their thoughtlessness by putting on glasses, the girls are whisked upward into the rafters.

Normally, this would be enough conversation piece to cap any show along the rialto, but the Lido show is full of pleasant surprises. The scenes unfold in sequence, all magnificent in colorful lighting, costumes, and with stirring music . . . capped by the glories of beautiful girls.

Being bashful by disposition tends to inhibit anything but professional analysis of the plentious expanse of anatomies presented, but from this layman's corner one can safely say that Pahrump will never be the same.

Stage sets such as this community has never witnessed rise and take form from the depths of the Stardust stage. Girls ride the props up, out of sight, water sequences with scores of pretty girls parading through exciting routines stir audience approval. In a shorter time than it takes to read about it . . . a water scene becomes an ice pad on which one of the show's principals, Jacqueline Du Bief, unlimbers some fancy footwork.

Throughout, acts of diverse nature but of uniformly high quality segment the show's production numbers. Gino Donati, Georges Campo with Lina Marvell, and Marvyn Roy all enjoy unstinted applause.

If one must single out an artist in the charm department, then that person must be Dorothea McFarland.

Credits should be voluminous. The work of Donn Arden speaks for itself, and to Frank Sennes goes thanks for efforts. Music for the show is by John Augustine.

As George Jessel observed, if we've left out anyone, or neglected to comment on what stood out in the minds of others, it probably stems from the trauma caused by the impact and enormity of "C'est Magnifique."

House lights dim, there's a few bars of overture, and from the ceiling of the Continental Cafe descend platforms, each with a bare-bosomed beauty, standing cool as you please, and before the surprise has caused nearsighted gentlemen to repair their thoughtlessness by putting on glasses, the girls are whisked upward into the rafters.

Normally, this would be enough conversation piece to cap any show along the rialto, but the Lido show is full of pleasant surprises. The scenes unfold in sequence, all magnificent in colorful lighting, costumes, and with stirring music . . . capped by the glories of beautiful girls.

Being bashful by disposition tends to inhibit anything but professional analysis of the plentious expanse of anatomies presented, but from this layman's corner one can safely say that Pahrump will never be the same.

rge Gobel attempts a yodel as his of my guitar" Marilyn Hanold lends dition during the comedian's open-

ike only happen in a Hollywood studio. No nightclub was ever built ood that could stage a show of such dimensions. The thing is a cinema fantasy. . there'll never BE a nightclub as big and as beautiful as these movie studio sets." And that's just where you were WRONG.

Cafe Continental, please, Sir.

The creative team behind several editions of Lido: *Madame Bluebell, who supplied a distinctive company of showgirls, American director-choreographer Donn Arden, center, and entertainment director Frank Sennes, right.*

the production shows in this town," Rader said. "This was the big one."

Arden also had a flair for spectacle in the form of re-creating disaster onstage. He was the bridge between Busby Berkeley and Irwin Allen, the producer of disaster movies such as *The Towering Inferno* and *The Poseidon Adventure*.

the Stardust in 1955 and occasionally worked there right up until its closing. And when he remembers the *Lido*, it's with palpable excitement.

"This was the hotel that was the start of all

"Each show had a spectacular (set piece)," said Len's wife, Jill, who was a *Lido* showgirl beginning in 1959. The second edition of *Lido*, she said, was the first to use a waterfall. She

also remembers that the waterfall built in Scotland wasn't a particular favorite of Arden. He said it was too loud. Another show depicted a mythical breaking of the Hoover Dam — inspired in part, she said, because "they had to use the water."

The seventh edition in 1967 offered a pirate adventure and "The Sinking of the Galleon." The 11th edition offered the "Eruption of Mount Fujiyama." The 12th (and what would be the final version in terms of production numbers) presented "Africa! Africa!" with elephants and "The Punishment of the Gods" with fire and water.

For years, the show was changed every year and a half, not just to keep customers coming back, but to keep from having to pay import taxes on the costumes and scenery. In fact, Fluff LeCoque — who worked for Arden in

A headpiece from the final edition of Lido *in front of a makeup mirror in the women's dressing room. Surviving costume pieces are scarce. For years, most of them were burned to avoid import taxes.*

One of the rare headpieces to survive the final edition of Lido, which ran from 1977 until the show closed in 1991. Most of the ornate costumes from previous revues were destroyed, though many found their way out the back door.

The headpiece from Enter the Night pays homage to classic showgirl style, but feathers were no longer augmented by fur as they were in the old days.

that era — remembers that at the end of each edition, all those gorgeous costumes made in Europe were "taken out into the desert and burned," under the watchful eyes of federal officials instead of paying the tariffs to send them back to France.

Len Rader remembers when a union dispute created a few bubbles.

"Somebody put Tide in the pool between the first and second shows," he said. "In those days, Tide was not a low-sudsing detergent."

The 12th edition, "Allez Lido," which debuted in January 1978, cost $2 million and turned out to be the last time the show had

The costumes made in Paris were "so glamorous," notes Fluff LeCoque, who worked for director Arden. "So many feathers and real fur, a lot of fox. You couldn't do that now."

The Stardust
Show Time

93

STARDUST

presents the fourth titanic edition direct from

LE LIDO DE PARIS
an astonishing all new revue
"VOILA!"
conceived and produced by **PIERRE LOUIS-GUERIN** and **RENE FRADAY**
staged and directed by **DONN ARDEN**

1. RENDEZVOUS DE PARIS
Les boulevardiers . . . . ARTHUR MAXWELL
                                JOHN JULIANO
Les demoiselles de Paris . . . . LES BLUEBELL GIRLS
Les Parisiens . . . . ARDEN BOY DANCERS
Les femmes chic . . . . . . LES BELLES DU LIDO
L'elegante . . . . **NICKY GORSKA**

2. VOILA LE LIDO
Les Miss Lido . . . . Mireille & Dagmar
Les presentateurs . . . . ARTHUR MAXWELL
                                JOHN JULIANO
                                ARDEN BOY DANCERS

3. HARMONIE AQUATIQUE
                          . . . **FLORENCE RAE**

THE DANCING WATERS

THE GREAT ICE STAGE

4. FEMMES ET DIAMANTS
a) Rue de la Paix:
   Les Chevaliers . . . . ARDEN BOY DANCERS
   Maurice . . . . ARTHUR MAXWELL
   Les femmes aux diamants . . LES BELLES DU LIDO
b) Le joyau magique:
   Le joyau . . . . LES BLUEBELL GIRLS

5. DEXTERITE . . . . **ERIC BRENN**

6. FANTAISIE D'ARABIE
a) Le marche:
   L'homme riche . . . . . . ARTHUR MAXWELL
   Les marchands . . . . LES BELLES DU LIDO
                                ARDEN BOY DANCERS
   L'homme de la rue . . . . . . JOHN JULIANO
   Les danseuses . . . . LES BLUEBELL GIRLS
   Les danseurs au sabre . . . ARDEN BOY DANCERS

Les esclaves . . . . LES BLUEBELL GIRLS
b) Les jarres mysterieuses: **ED. SEIFERT AND CO.**
c) Le harem du sultan:
   Le sultan . . . . ARTHUR MAXWELL
   La princesse . . . . **NICKY GORSKA**
   Les favorites . . . . . . LES BELLES DU LIDO
d) Parade orientale:
   La garde du sultan . . . . LES BLUEBELL GIRLS
                                ARDEN BOY DANCERS

7. ILLUSIONS . . . . **GERD MARON**

8. LA VALLEE EN PERIL
a) The control room:
   Francois . . . . ARTHUR MAXWELL
   Pierre . . . . JOHN JULIANO
b) La tragedie:

AMAZING FLOOD EFFECT

9. SURPRISES . . . . **DICK ALBERT**

10. L'OPERA DE PARIS
a) Le grand staircase:
   Les opera goers . . . . **ARTHUR MAXWELL**
                                JOHN JULIANO

   Aida . . . . Kathy
   Faust . . . . Mireille
   La Boheme . . . . NICKY GORSKA
   La Traviata . . . . Pierette
   La Walkyrie . . . . FLORENCE RAE
   Le Chevalier a la rose . . . . Sylvia
   Les contes d'Hoffman . . . . Antoinette
b) Moment symphonique: . . . . . . **LES NITWITS**
c) Bal de Gala:

THE FIREWORKS

Grand finale . . . . . TOUTE LA COMPAGNIE

Show supervision **FRANK SENNES** / Costumes created by **FOLCO**
Sets designed by Harvey Warren and Fost / Art direction Harvey Warren
Original Music by Landreau, Brienne, Betti & Delvincourt
All costumes made in Paris by Karinska, Turpin, Marinette-Aumont
Vicaire, Lebrun & Falk. Men's formals by Faivret.
Assistants to Donn Arden: Ffolliott Chorlton & Wisa D'Orso
Captain for girls: Tony Haineline — for boys: Rod Bieber
Interiors of Cafe Continental created and designed by Jac Lessman
Company Manager: Bill De Angelis

EDDIE O'NEIL
and his orchestra

SHOW TIMES
8:15 and 12 Midnight / 2:30 a.m. Saturday

a top-to-bottom overhaul. As costs escalated and Las Vegas slumped in the early 1980s, the producers took the different tactic of giving headline billing to Siegfried & Roy, then Bobby Berosini, rather than changing the production numbers.

The Showgirl's Life

Lido had about 60 performers, and the majority of them were female. In the early days, the showgirls were assembled and overseen by Madame Bluebell, a French choreographer known for not hiring any women under 5 feet 9 inches tall, the point where most classical ballerinas would be

The 1975 edition of **Lido** *included* **Banana Town** *as part of an extended sequence entitled* **South America, Take it Away!**

Bright Lights & Wedding Bells

Like so many others, Len Rader didn't plan to settle in Las Vegas.

He came to town on vacation, back in the late '50s. He'd heard they were short of spotlight operators, and that was something Rader had done in Fresno, California. Rader went to work at the Tropicana, then the Desert Inn and finally the Stardust.

Then he fell in love. Jill Gladman was a *Lido* showgirl who hadn't planned to settle in Las Vegas either. One night, stage manager Bill DeAngelis gave a party for cast and crew at the Black Magic at Tropicana Avenue and Paradise Road. At the party, Len went up to Jill to ask her if she thought her roommate would go out with him. Somehow, he never did end up dating the roommate.

"Suddenly, we're going to get married," Jill recalls, despite her earlier scorn: "What, me marry an American? You've got to be joking."

But the big obstacle turned out to be the Catholic Church. Len was a Catholic; Jill had been baptized but not confirmed.

"Father Crowley — he took care of it," Jill Rader said.

Father Richard Crowley was a priest who was a friend to the entertainment community in Las Vegas, regularly conducting mass at the Old Frontier. A friend by that time, he arranged for another priest to hear her confession. She took her first Holy Communion there after the third show, at about 5 a.m. on February 14, 1960. They were married that afternoon.

They asked if they could have the reception in the *Lido* band room. After the first show, she remembers, "we rushed back to the apartment and we started to make sandwiches. We went back and changed after the second show."

DeAngelis had the whole stage transformed.

"He had taken care of everything for us," she said. "We had sandwiches. We had a lot of buffet stuff. It was a fabulous reception. The only family and friends we had was the company. And of course they all came."

Right, Len and Jill Rader recreate their 1960 wedding day on the Stardust stage. Opposite and left: Jill's snapshots of her showgirl days.

considered too tall.

Between them, Arden and Bluebell created an Americanized version of the showgirl. "There's a certain way a girl can walk, particularly when you're going across the stage," Arden noted in a 1989 interview included in the book *The First 100: Portraits of the Men and Women Who Shaped Las Vegas.*

"By simply twisting the foot, it swings the pelvis forward, which is suggestive and sensual. If you twist right and swing that torso, you get a revolve going in there that's just right. It isn't the way a woman should walk, necessarily, unless she's a hooker. You're selling the pelvis; that's the Arden Walk."

"These ladies were something we'd never seen before," Len Rader said. "Wonderful smiles. I just kind of melted. When the girls came over from Paris, it was so unique, these tall showgirls and dancers."

"We came over on special talent visas," said Jill Rader. "A lot of us didn't have any special talents, but we were tall."

The former Jill Gladman grew up in England and worked as a showgirl in London for five years. She toured with Madame Bluebell for two tours of Italy.

Then Jill was asked if she'd like to come to Las Vegas.

"I promptly said 'No,' " she remembers. "I

The "Africa! Africa!" segment in 1978 included The Elephants of Ketchell, who had to hang out somewhere out back when they weren't onstage.

Medieval Mishaps

Lido de Paris was usually a very smooth, polished show, but it wasn't without its mishaps. Rena Warden, a showgirl from 1969 through 1979, remembers two.

In one scene, showgirls and dancers in medieval costumes would parade around the stage, then go sit in a box with other cast members. A performer on a white horse (the show's main adagio lead) and a horse trainer on a black horse would come in on the premise of "entertaining" the cast members in the boxes. One night, however, there was a replacement horse. A particularly long-legged replacement horse.

"It was supposed to run around a partition onto the stage," Warden remembers. "It slipped on the concrete backstage." There was a long table in the showroom, perpendicular to the stage.

"It plowed onto the table," Warden said. "It got to the end of the table and stood up. Then the horse ran up the center aisle.

"We heard about a lawsuit, but we don't know how it ended up. They hushed things like that up. You have to remember the Mob was there."

On another night, a performer named Gloria Tiffany, who rode down from the rafters on a large disc, slid off of it and onto a guest table. A guest was hurt, Warden said, and so was Tiffany.

"You could see an imprint of a Stardust ashtray on her thigh," Warden said. "You could see the little part where the cigarette goes."

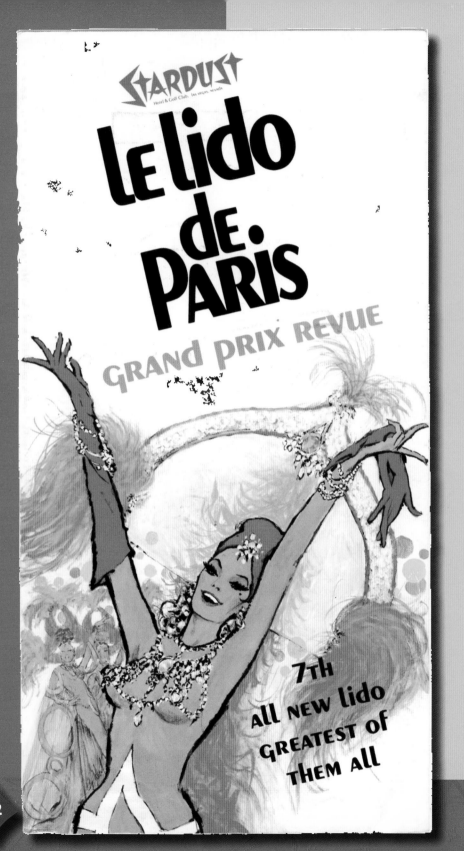

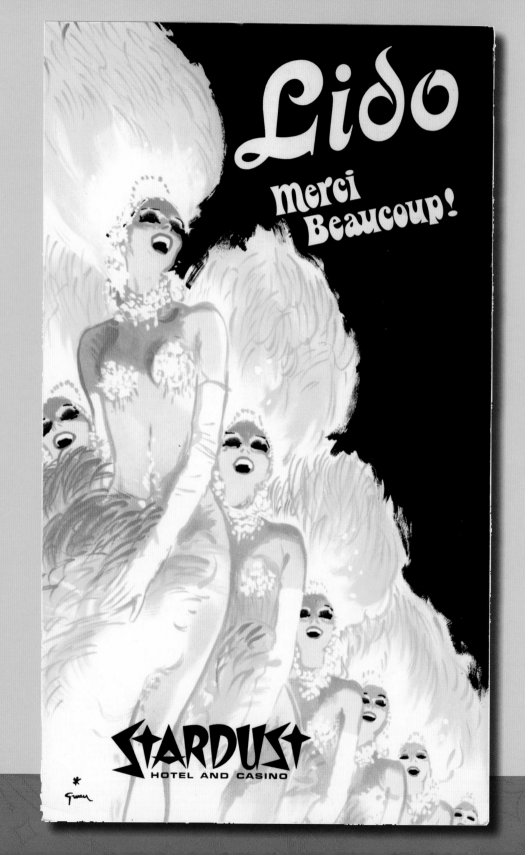

The All New **Lido de Paris** Direct From Paris!

The only show in Las Vegas imported from Paris with its original cast...to the American home of the "Lido de Paris," at the

STARDUST
HOTEL AND CASINO
LAS VEGAS

Adieu Lido

Lido *programs throughout the years. Page 101: Variant covers for the 12th edition. The one on the right came after Siegfried & Roy were added to the show, but before they were featured on the cover. Page 102: The 1967 edition, left, and the 11th edition, circa 1975. Above left, another cover for the 12th edition, crediting Frank Rosenthal as "director of entertainment" inside. Above, a special program printed for the Lido's closing . Next page: Alternate cover for the 11th edition.*

said I'd rather go to the *Lido* in Paris. "They said it would be a way to see America. But Las Vegas is not typical of America," and she had some inkling of that from a film she'd seen.

Three or four months later, she was persuaded to make the trip.

The *Lido* casts always arrived from Paris together. The first show ran for 11 months; the second, in which Jill performed, ran for 16 months.

"Very few of us had flown before," she said.

They left Paris on a charter flight on an old

plane. "I notice they didn't use it to go back," she quipped.

They stopped in New York, for an appearance on a game show. The show's first prize was a trip to Las Vegas with the *Lido* performers.

After maybe 48 hours in New York, they took off for Chicago, then on to Las Vegas after a brief stop. The plane flew low, she remembers, and it was extremely hot on board. The cast members, comfortable with displaying their bodies, removed their tops in an effort to cool off.

"Except for the lead nude," she said. "She took everything off."

And the poor game-show winner, a young man from the Midwest, turned several shades of red.

At long last they landed in Las Vegas.

"It was hot and dusty," she said. She remembers being shocked by seeing people openly gambling, even though she knew to expect it.

Their respite after arrival would be brief. After two or three hours of sleep, it was time for rehearsal. Jill Rader remembers lying down in a showroom booth to rest, and noticing something sort of odd under the table.

"Look at all the bumps under here," she told a friend.

"It's chewing gum," was the reply. One more bit of culture shock.

Whenever they were seen in public, the performers had to have their hair done, makeup perfect.

"It's like the old movie stars — glammed up," Jill Rader said.

And they were quite the attraction at the Big Dipper pool.

"Well, we all had bikinis on," she said. "People would ask to take pictures."

The sense of extended family appealed to Rena Warden, a *Lido* showgirl from 1969 to 1979. A native of Connecticut, she'd studied dance with Martha Graham before hitchhiking to California at age 19. She'd seen a cover of *Life* magazine. "They had this pot of gold and this rainbow. Plus, my brother was there."

She went to work at May Co., where she met her future husband.

"Of course I had my eye on him, because he was 6'3"," said the 6-foot-tall Warden.

She taught tap and ballet. "And then somebody said to me, 'You have to get into show business.' " She answered a Moro Landis ad.

"They went nuts for this 6-footer," Warden said. She was dancing in San Francisco when fellow dancer Don Courey advised her to go to Las Vegas.

Warden was in a show at another casino for a few months but found the girls a little too jaded; "it wasn't my cup of tea."

In September 1969, she went to see *Lido de Paris* producer Frank Sennes and tried the brash approach.

"Why don't you fire one of those fat broads and hire me?" Warden asked

The massive headdresses worn by Lido showgirls were difficult to balance.

him.

He did.

"It was perfect for me," Warden said. Her two sons were already with her, and her husband moved to Las Vegas.

Most of the Bluebell Girls were in their late teens, Warden said. And Miss Bluebell ran a pretty tight ship.

"They were nice girls," Warden said. "The girls weren't as sassy or snooty" as in some other shows.

"Showgirls were in the same dressing rooms as the dancers," she said, "so there was a lot of snobbery going on back there."

Warden performed in four shows, which by that time were 2½ years each. The costumes came over from Paris before the beginning of each new show, she said.

"They took personalities into account when designing," Warden said. "Your name was in it when it came from Paris. The costumes had to be really well made, because they had to last 2½ years."

The beaded costumes were often very heavy, Warden said, and frequently included large, ornate headpieces, which were not only heavy but also very difficult to balance.

"Once you had it down it was OK," she said, "and we had it down by opening night."

Warden remembers one particular headdress that was so tall, she had to duck while passing beneath one piece of scenery.

" Stop! Stop! "she remembers Arden yelling. "So they had to change the scenery."

Tears Flow for Final Bow

The "Lido de Paris" came to Las Vegas as an immigrant in 1958. It leaves town next Thursday, after 32 ½ years, as a naturalized citizen.

That loss of its foreign identity, and the price of restoring it, may well be what ultimately led to its death.

The formal reasons for the "Lido" leaving the Stardust deal with matters of budget and artistic control. But those reasons tie back to the notion that the "Lido" outlasted the benefits of paying for its historic name.

When the "Lido" opened at the Stardust on July 2, 1958, the imported cast of eyecatching showgirls came with the exotic trappings of the French nightclub show: feathers, sequins and -- ou la la! -- female upper nudity.

But something curious happened over the next 32 ½ years. A visit to any souvenir shop on the Strip will bear it out: That striking showgirl image has evolved into a symbol of Las Vegas, not Paris.

"(Stardust owner) The Boyd Group came to realize they were spending an awful lot of money for a name that wasn't doing them any good anymore," said one local entertainment analyst.

Unlike the Tropicana Hotel's "Les Folies Bergere" -- which pays a licensing fee to use the name but produces the show itself -- "Lido" shows are produced in France, then moved to the Stardust. All changes must be authorized in Paris.

A sadder notion is that the cost of bringing the "Lido" back to the standards of its French counterpart is more than what most Las Vegas hotels are likely to spend these days.

The current edition of the Paris "Lido" cost $8 million; few hotels these days would be likely to spend even the $727,500 that it cost to revamp the "Lido" in 1973 ($300,000 of it on costumes alone), much less what the purchasing power of that sum would equal today.

"The budget is perhaps larger than what (The Boyd Group) would have anticipated, said Burton Brown, the liaison between Las Vegas and the "Lido" headquarters in Paris.

Both sides say they are parting amicably, but both are ready to go their separate ways after years of start-and-stop efforts to overhaul the "Lido."

"The Stardust wants more direct artistic control over the show, so if the market changes, they could alter the show at their whim," Brown says.

"We have a (expanded and remodeled) hotel that's headed in a new marketing direction, and we thought it was time for something new," Stardust publicist Kathy Espin said.

In a letter from Paris, the director general of the "Lido" organization explained, "We just had different points of view with the new management of the Stardust and we both agreed it was time for a change."

But the director, Pierre Lissillour, also said "there are plans to move the *Lido* to another hotel in Las Vegas or elsewhere in the United States. ... People from other countries also came to us. A few projects are realistic."

Less realistic is finding a hotel that will front the money for the kind of show that has long been associated with the "Lido" name. The Stardust show has stagnated as decisions to revitalize it kept getting postponed.

"It's a very tired show," Brown acknowledges. "It's not representative of what we would like people to know as the *Lido*."

The 12th and current version, "Allez Lido," opened on Dec. 23, 1977. The music and choreography have not changed since, though the costumes are not the originals and some frills -- such as live elephants in the African sequence -- have disappeared from the show. The Stardust's advertising now centers on

March 2, 1991 ★ ★ a

PEOPLE

DAWN TERESE
The showgirl and other cast members of the "Lido de Paris" revue take their final bows.
Page 1B

headliner Bobby Berosini, not the revue itself.

Donn Arden, the revue's choreographer since its inception, says he was twice denied the opportunity to revamp the "Lido," in 1983 and 1987.

Each edition was supposed to have a maximum run of four years, Arden said by telephone from his Palm Springs, Calif., home recently. After working several months on preproduction elements such as music and costume design, he says he was told both times that "because of the financial condition of the times (the hotel) couldn't afford the expenditure."

Arden made the "Lido" and Bally's "Jubilee!" famous for massive props and lavish spectacle. "An Arden show, as everyone knows, is expensive," he says.

Arden's contract with the Stardust led to an apparent stalemate over the years. He says he would prefer to remain in semi-retirement than stage a smaller-scale production: "I won't do a cheap show."

The "Lido" was renewed every year for its first three years, then basically in two-year stretches throughout the 1960s. Gradually the chorus featuring the internationally famous "Bluebell Girls" became more Americanized.

"After 1972 it seemed more Americans came in," says veteran dancer Sharon Smith. When she joined the show that year, there were only four or five American members. U.S. immigration laws eventually barred the use of any foreign performers without a permanent resident "green card," she said.

One of the "Lido's" lead showgirls was Valerie Perrine, who went on to win an Oscar for her role in "Lenny." (The 1968 program lists her in a "Phantom of the Opera" sequence that came years before the Andrew Lloyd Webber version). Another was the fictional Harmony, the main character in Larry McMurtry's "The Desert Rose." The 1983 novel dealt with the consequences of the aging showgirl being replaced by her own daughter.

Just how closely the Stardust's new show -- due in July -- will resemble the "Lido" in concept or budget remains to be seen. The hotel might opt for a contemporary theme, judging from casting notices that call for a "Sting"-type male lead and dancers versed in "hip-hop."

A contemporary show, coincidentally, is cheaper. "The whole world has changed, so has Vegas," Arden notes. "Today all you need is a pair of torn blue jeans and one feather."

by Mike Weatherford
This article first appeared in the
Las Vegas Review-Journal on February 22, 1991

Dawn Terese, a showgirl at the "Lido de Paris" show, wipes a tear from her eye while standing backstage after the final performance of the Stardust Hotel show on Thursday night.

Jeff Scheid/Review-Journal

Performers cry, hug at 'Lido' finale

☐ Some dancers hold back tears during the show's first number as the revue concludes a 32-year run.

By Mike Weatherford
Review-Journal

"This is it, babe," said Kim DeSantis, extending a hug to lead carpenter Stan Melvin before taking her place one last time behind the curtain of the "Lido de Paris."

DeSantis' prediction that there would be "a lot of eyelashes crying down the face" came true within minutes of Thursday night's final performance. Some dancers were choking back tears in the opening number as they circled the passarela in the Stardust Hotel showroom.

Just above stage right — near the portal where the cheesy "satellites" came out of dry dock to make one more turn over the heads of the audience — was a sign of the future: A stylized poster announcing the Stardust's new show, "Enter the Night," to open July 15.

Many "Lido" crew members, including company manager Terry Lovern, already are at work on the new show. And several dancers auditioned for it last week. "It seemed like the right thing to do," Linda LeBourveau, the longest tenured cast member, said. She's been with the "Lido" off and on since 1970, but said, "I'm still feeling pretty spunky."

But Thursday was more a night for looking back on the Strip's oldest revue. The invited-guest audience was packed with "Lido" vet show's opening

On an average night, the "Lido" cast would be content to perform to blank-faced tourists who save their occasional applause for the specialty acts. On Thursday, the audience of friends and family members cheered and applauded every change of scenery and each bit of choreography.

"The feeling generated inside the theater was spectacular," said Robert Boughner, the Boyd Group's executive vice president, who claims to have seen the revue 351 times.

"Everyone was working extra hard and the energy was wonderful," said Janet Kravenko, who was in the show in 1959. She was there with her two daughters — who both danced in later editions of the "Lido."

Lido

From 1B

Alison Gesmundo, who joined the show in 1986.

After the show, the cast and audience adjourned to a party set up for 1,000 in the Stardust's new convention center. The speech-making lasted until midnight, when a host of former "Bluebell Girl" dancers linked arms around choreographer Donn Arden while Doug Gardiner sang "Auld Lang Syne."

The guest list included magicians Siegfried and Roy, who worked for both the Stardust "Lido" and its Paris counterpart for nine years before leaving in 1981 to star in their own revue.

"I always said the "Lido" was the best showcase for any act," said Siegfried Fishbacher. "If you could say you worked for the "Lido," you could work all over the world for the rest of your life."

The "Lido" is the show that "el-evated Las Vegas entertainment to what it is today," Roy Horn added.

Bill Boyd, the Boyd Group's chief executive officer, cleared up weeks of back-and-forth hedging by announcing Bobby Berosini would indeed be part of the new show. Berosini thanked Boyd Group officials for "standing behind their performer," during the time his orangutan act was under fire from animal rights activists.

Arden, the revue's choreographer since the show opened, was upbeat despite his contention he still has a contract with the Stardust. His only dig was saying, "I think the "Lido" made the Stardust."

Stardust officials might find that hard to argue. As Burton Brown, the show's liaison with its French counterpart noted, the "Lido" came to town on a six-month contract and stayed more than 32 years. "I guess we must have been a hit," he said.

Lounge around the world

When the Stardust advertised "continuous entertainment" in its lounge, it wasn't kidding around.

Like the Sands, Sahara and other classic-Vegas destinations, the lounge was a vital part of the legend. The showroom attraction drew the players to the casino; the lounges kept them there until dawn. But the Stardust had the only lounge with a revolving stage. As soon as one act would finish a set, someone pushed a button and the stage wheeled around in a half circle to reveal the next act's drum kit and microphones ready to go.

The Stardust's roster was a particu-

The Kim Sisters learned to sing in English — at first by phonetically mimicking records — and eventually mastered more than 10 musical instruments each during their 14 years at the Stardust.

larly exotic lineup. Perhaps the hotel was taking a cue from the international flavor of *Lido de Paris* and the Aku Aku restaurant, or maybe it was just coincidence. Three of the most popular and enduring acts were the Kim Sisters — a Korean sibling act in the vein of the McGuire Sisters — "Hawaiian charmer" Nalani Kele and her Polynesian revue, and Juan Garcia Esquivel, the Mexican band leader whose quirky, bongo-laden compositons were marketed simply as Esquivel! by RCA Records in the early days of stereo.

Esquivel was rediscovered during the retro/swing revial of the 1990s, when his music was cleverly repackaged with the title *Space Age Bachelor*

Pad Music. A genuine space-age bachelor himself — or at least a four-times-married ladies' man — the late band leader explained in 1997 that the focus of his Stardust act wasn't so much the tuned

Suave bandleader Juan Esquivel put together an unusual lounge show that included synchronized lighting, tuned percussion instruments and four female singers of different nationalities.

percussion or synchronized light show, but the four female singers he took great care in choosing. "Every girl was a different nationality . . . I had them dressed so smartly," he recalled.

"They were dressed in such a way that at one point, they tore their dresses with the Velcro material and they would show their legs. Not to be nude, of course, but they would show enough to attract the boys."

The Kim Sisters also attracted their share of "boys," even though the three were still teenagers when they began working the Stardust in 1959. Sue Kim says that when men would ask one of them to go off and drink or dine with them, they would tell him, "Three go or no go."

The sisters had a dramatic journey to Las Vegas. In South Korea, their father was an orchestra conductor assasinated by the North Koreans at the start of the Korean war. Their

Nalani Kele's Polynesian Revue offered a mini-production show that tied into the exotic trappings of the casino's popular Aku Aku restaurant.

mother was left with seven children, and, struggling to make ends meet, taught them to sing a song in English to entertain U.S. troops. "The G.I.s loved us. We couldn't learn the next song fast enough," Sue recalls. If the troops rewarded them with whiskey or beer, the teens would exchange it for rice on the black market.

Word of the sister act traveled back to the States with returning servicemen and came to the attention of an agent, who in 1959 flew to Korea to sign them

for the Thunderbird's *China Doll Revue*: "20 of the most beautiful Oriental showgirls ever assembled on the same stage," the ads proclaimed. When that revue ran its eight-week course, 17-year-old Sue and sisters Mia and Aija moved to the Stardust lounge.

They worked from 1 a.m. until 7 a.m., playing six half-hour sets each night. They would walk back and forth to the one-bedroom apartment they shared near the Sahara hotel. "We would go home and sleep, get up and practice," Sue recalls. They listened to English re-cords and learned the lyrics phonetically. "We didn't know what the hell we were singing."

And the language barrier didn't help them the night they got stuck on the re-volving stage, going around in circles. "We didn't know how to ask how this thing works," she remembers with a laugh.

When Ed Sullivan came to the Stardust to broadcast his TV show from the *Lido* stage in 1962, he fell for the sisters and put them on his show for the first

of 22 appearances. The lounge rotation also included more conventional Vegas-style musical comedy with the Novelites, crooners Don Cornell and Billy Daniels and even a mni-revue, *Bare Touch of Vegas.*

Esquivel stayed at the Stardust lounge until 1971. The sisters moved to the Las Vegas Hilton in 1973. The original lounge closed on September 15, 1975, incorporated into the design of an enlarged and expanded casino. A year later, the casino opened the larger Starlight Theatre Lounge in a new location. The bigger room allowed for bigger names, including Fats Domino and Eartha Kitt. Another small revue called *Tickle Your Fancy* featured the confetti-tossing king of camp, Rip Taylor. A

casino dealer and lounge singer named Lee Greenwood would later move up to the big time by recording the patriotic modern-day standard, *God Bless The U.S.A.*

Sue Kim says she cried when they tore down the Thunderbird, so she can't even imagine how it willl feel to lose the Stardust. "It was the best thing that ever happened to us."

— Mike Weatherford (Author of *Cult Vegas — The Weirdest! The Wildest! The Swingin'est Town on Earth!*)

Over the years, the Stardust lounge showcased some big names, some local heroes and a few who would go on to bigger fame. From top left to right: Don Cornell in 1971, A Bare Touch of Vegas in 1974, The Novelites in 1970, Eartha Kitt in 1976 and Lee Greenwood in 1975.

Music of the Years

A new era, a new show and a Midnight Idol

Enter the Night *had a teasing, contemporary title and poster art to match. It also was the rare Las Vegas show to sell a soundtrack album of its original score.*

Enter the Nineties

Hotel officials let the local show business community play a guessing game about a replacement for *Lido* until the old gal had her last hurrah and bowed out with all due ceremony on February 28, 1991. Once the final curtain fell, however, Boyd executive

Robert Boughner explained plans for a new review called *Enter the Night* to *Las Vegas Review-Journal* columnist Michael Paskevich.

"I can tell you it's not going to look like a typical burlesque (or) vaudeville format where it's production number, curtain act, production number, curtain act," Boughner noted. "We got so many (proposed) shows that looked just like that."

Instead, producer Ted Lorenz — a newcomer to the Strip — sold the company on his vision of infusing the showgirl revue with a Broadway sensibility. There would be no lip-syncing to hokey, old-fashioned music. The lead singers would wear headset microphones and make eye contact with one another while performing original songs.

"The challenge of revues

is making contact with the audience," Lorenz noted. "Most revues don't make contact until the juggler comes out . . . We're committed to live performance. Real singers singing songs. Real dancers dancing."

If the title didn't let audiences know this wasn't the *Lido*, the show opening did. Instead of bombarding the audience with the entire 62-member cast, a lone singer, Marilyn Kaye, emerged from a foggy side

STARRING
BOBBY BEROSINI'S ORANGUTANS

Bobby Berosini: The Fur Flies

Today, many remember Bobby Berosini mainly for a protracted legal battle with People for the Ethical Treatment of Animals. But in his heyday, Berosini and his orangutans helped focus the national spotlight on the Stardust.

Berosini, born Bohumil Berousek, came from a Czechoslovakian family that had been circus performers for generations. He and his wife, Joan, eventually made it to Las Vegas as a specialty act performing with three orangutans and two chimpanzees. His Las Vegas career paralled and sometimes followed that of Siegfried & Roy. Like the magical duo, he and his orangutans worked in the MGM Grand Hotel Revues *Hallelujah, Hollywood!* and Bally's *Jubilee.* They were drafted as *Lido* headliners to replace Siegfried & Roy in early 1984, after the magical duo's departure for their own show at the Frontier caused *Lido* attendance to sag.

They had prominent billing on the Stardust's landmark neon sign and even on the show's programs. The little primates brought an air of levity — and, some say, much-needed comic relief — to the show. Their gestures were

designed to poke fun at their human audience, even at Berosini himself.

"You have to make sure everything they do is perceived as fun, not work, and never give them a task to perform that they will come to resent after a while," Berosini told *Review-Journal* reporter Pete Mikla soon after he joined the *Lido*.

And they were known far beyond Las Vegas. Berosini trained the orangutan for the Clint Eastwood movie *Every Which Way But Loose*, and in 1985, he and the little guys entertained President Ronald and Nancy Reagan in a *All-Star Salute to Ford's Theater*, which was broadcast on CBS. *The New York Times* reported that the Reagans could be seen "howling at the devilish antics of Bobby Berosini's orangutans, one of which flashes what is called a Jimmy Carter smile."

Eventually, outside forces intervened to render any creative issues moot. Berosini left the show after animal rights activists rallied around a video purporting to show Berosini beating one of his orangutans. Berosini claimed the tape was doctored, but the damage done by repeated news airings of the footage and worldwide coverage of the controversy was irreparable.

Suits and counter-suits — and multiple court decisions — followed. But what really may have sealed the fate of Berocini and the orangutans on the Strip was the transition from the more traditional variety style of *Lido de Paris* to the new Las Vegas and its dominance by the animal-free *Cirque du Soleil*.

When Lido *gave way to* Enter the Night, *the Stardust retained Berosini as headliner and tried to give him a make-over inspired by Siegfried & Roy's Zen-like relationship with their animals. But the act itself didn't change, and never quite blended with the new show.*

To combat the loss of Siegfried & Roy's tigers, the Lido *recruited another animal act. But unlike the tigers, Bobby Berosini's orangutans were known to flip the bird.*

At times, such as the "Some Like It Hot" number, Enter the Night *realized its ambitious goal of updating showgirls to a 1990s context.*

stage to croon the atmospheric title song.

The $10 million production included a total overhaul of the showroom's light and sound system, even new upholstery on the booths. But one key element of *Lido* did carry over as a link to the past: Bobby Berosini and his orangutans.

Review-Journal critic Paskevich found it an awkward mix when the show opened in August 1991. "By updating the production-show genre with Broadway-styled theatrics, producer Ted Lorenz and company have come up with the best new show of the year," he wrote.

However, he thought Berosini's act "simply doesn't mesh with the contemporary, stylized look of the rest of the show . . . Depending on your viewpoint, Berosini and his furry buddies either lift the affair with welcome humor or nearly wreck it in a 27-minute tour de force of bad taste."

Eventually, outside forces intervened to render any creative issues moot. Berosini left the show after animal rights activists rallied

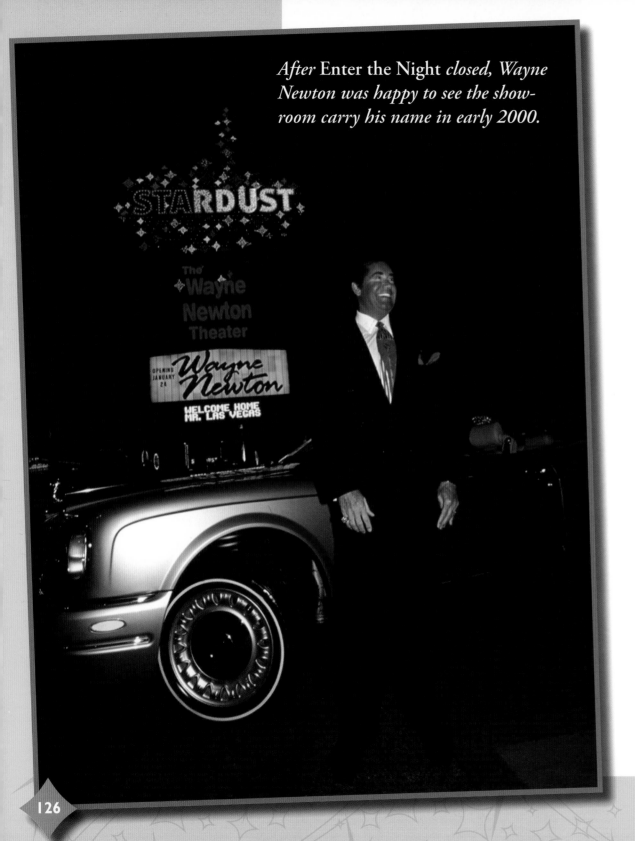

After Enter the Night *closed, Wayne Newton was happy to see the showroom carry his name in early 2000.*

around a video purporting to show Berosini beating one of his orangutans. Berosini claimed the tape was doctored, but the damage done by repeated news airings of the footage and worldwide coverage of the controversy was irreparable.

Exit the 'Night,' Welcome the 'Midnight Idol'

For a couple of years, *Enter the Night* was ahead of the curve when it came to reinventing the Las Vegas production show. When the show fired on all cylinders — such as a thumping rendition of the Robert Palmer hit *Some Like It Hot* that exploded with crimson plumage, cheeky choreography and pyrotechnic effects — the producers' vision was vindicated.

But the vision proved short-sighted. No one could have foreseen that a sea change in Las Vegas entertainment was on the horizon. Two and a half years after the show debuted, Cirque du Soleil opened *Mystere* at Treasure Island and redefined the aesthetic for a Las Vegas

spectacle.

Ironically, *Enter the Night* had lured away a Cirque aerialist named Vladimir. But on all other counts, $10 million suddenly didn't seem like a lot of money compared with *Mystere* and its $92 million follow-up, *O* at Bellagio. The Stardust revue did solid business for the run of the decade but, like the hotel as a whole, dropped from the

Natalie Oliver, left, was one of the talented singers that lent a Broadway feel to the new revue, which tried to fight the lip-syncing of older showroom productions.

Becoming A Showgirl

She was Aki, "a showgirl for the 21st century," promoted by the Stardust as the star of *Enter the Night* on billboards and even on the tail of a Western Pacific Airlines jet. But for showgirl-turned-attorney Akee Levin, "it was all very boring."

Levin says that with a laugh, and more than a trace of fondness. She didn't, you see, exactly set out to become a showgirl.

"I, like I think most showgirls, came from a classical background," Levin said. "What happens is you start auditioning and there's not that many ballet companies. I'm five (foot)-nine, so on pointe shoes I would be six (foot)-something. They like those ballerinas really, really tiny. Very few possibilities exist for classically trained tall dancers."

Levin, a native of the Netherlands, saw two career choices.

"You can work for some kind of modern company, and you do this kind of weird modern stuff," she said. "My friends would go to these companies and be basically on unemployment and work just for the love of dance, which is great, but I just didn't like that whole idea of modern companies."

The other alternative: become a showgirl. Levin's choice was made: "I'm gonna go to Paris and work for a show there (and) still try to break into some kind of a (ballet) company," she figured.

"Then I realized that being in a show was not so bad. You didn't have to be ridiculously skinny and your feet didn't hurt from the pointe shoes. I started to really enjoy it and I liked the people. This was really fun."

She spent seven years with the famed Crazy Horse Saloon in Paris. While there, she started doing promotional work, going to Hong Kong and posing for photos to promote the show.

She came to Las Vegas on a 1995 vacation. She wanted to meet Terry Lovern, who was company manager for *Enter the Night* at the Stardust. The introduction was arranged by a mutual friend, Russell Plasko, who was now working as head of wardrobe for *Enter the Night* .

"He said, 'I talked to Terry. He doesn't want to meet you, he wants you to audition,'" she remembers.

She also remembers not feeling prepared for an audition, due to something that's tripped up a lot of visitors to Las Vegas. "I'd just been visiting the buffet at Treasure Is-

land," Levin said. "I didn't feel like I was in shape. But I was still at the Crazy Horse then, so I must have been."

She auditioned.

"He had this vision. He said, 'I think you come from a totally different kind of show. It would be great to have you come from Paris and introduce you and have a special number made around you.'"

She remembers weeks of talks. Lovern was telling her, "I want you to come as a star."

"I'm like, 'You know what, I don't care. Let me just be in the chorus. I don't need to be a principal dancer.' "

Oh, but Lovern had other plans.

"I started in June," she said. "Three weeks later, I was literally doing pictures for the billboards. That's how

fast it was — boom!

During the billboard era, she said, "they decided they were going to do a logojet. At the end they put me on a bus."

But she didn't plan on being a showgirl forever, star or not. Levin already had been studying Dutch law through a correspondence program with a Dutch university.

She had planned to go back to the Netherlands, but also thought she'd like to live in the United States. "I really liked Las Vegas already then," she said. "And by that time I'd been gone for so long from Holland.

"In retrospect, the Dutch law degree came in very handy. I went straight to law school," without being required to take any pre-law courses.

And the law school she attended? The Wil-

liam S. Boyd School of Law at the University of Nevada, Las Vegas.

"It was so nice. Amazing, just this whole turn of events. I'm working for him, basically, and he starts that law school and I'm already thinking, 'Hmm, maybe I could do that.' "

Levin said she saw Boyd at a few functions while she was in law school.

"He told me, 'You'll have to tell me when you graduate; I want to come.' I thought, 'Yeah, right.' "

But when Levin graduated, summa cum laude, Boyd was there.

"He made a speech," she said. "He said, 'Before I start my (prepared) speech, I want to acknowledge Akee Levin. She was a big star at the Stardust and from what I've seen, she's a big star in your law school.' It was very moving for me."

Today, Levin's an attorney in Las Vegas, and still keeps in contact with Lovern and a few other friends from *Enter the Night*. And she is wistful about the demise of the Stardust.

"I think it's always sad, because they tear every (aging) hotel down," she said.

"But sometimes you just need to go with the times. Thank God for the pictures we have."

got beer?

Aki was the cover girl for a a Boyd Gaming promotional publication advertising its Triple 7 brewpub at sister property Main Street Station.

Aki, Showgirl for the 21st Century
Stardust's "Enter the Night"
Preferred Beer: High Roller Gold

"People think showgirls are health food fanatics. We are for the most part, but I'm from Holland and back there beer *is* health food. The Triple 7 has the best in town."

"must-see" list to a more value-focused middle tier. *Enter the Night* closed at the end of 1999 after 4,435 performances.

Dynamic ice skater Burt Lancon had performed in both *Lido* and *Enter the Night*. "I'm excited, a bit nostalgic, but not sad," he told a backstage reporter on closing night. "I'm 39 years old, and at that age, Spandex is a privilege, not a right." Nonetheless, he echoed the sentiments for the earlier revue when he said, "It's the end of a great era."

In light of the changes on the Strip, the decision to pursue a little star power and sign an icon of middle America was a sound idea at the time. In October 1999, the Stardust called a press conference to announce the signing of Wayne Newton for 40 weeks per year in the re-named Wayne Newton Theater.

Name Recognition

"Christmas came awfully early," Newton said of a deal that came after years of contentious relationships with theater partners in Branson, Missouri. The deal was rumored to be worth as much as $25 million per year. Newton called it "the most lucrative contract I have ever signed." Amazingly, as he pointed out, he was only the third show in the Stardust's history.

The singer, who was 57 at the time, rang in a new century at the Stardust on

"After Wayne, we booked star shows, which is something kind of unique for now for Las Vegas," Bill Boyd said. "I think there are still people who would like to come in and see their favorite singer or comedian."

Headliners included Las Vegas veterans Don Rickles, Ann-Margret, B.B. King, the comedy team of Tim Conway and Harvey Korman, George Carlin, Bob Newhart, the band *Chicago* and the teamed-up *Temptations* and *Four Tops*. The most unusual booking may have been movie star Kevin Spacey, doing a tribute to Bobby Darin in December 2004, cross-promoting his Darin movie bio *Beyond the Sea*.

The Stardust found itself in the news in August 2004 when the Cuban revue *Havana*

New Year's weekend. But once he dug in for a regular schedule, he continued to battle vocal problems that had plagued him for the past decade. After the terrorist attacks of September 11, 2001, Newton spent more time pursuing his calling to entertain U.S. troops through the United Service Organizations.

That left more openings in the schedule to book other headliners, which were becoming a fading tradition on the Strip.

SPECIAL HOLIDAY PERFORMANCES
THE MAGIC OF
RICK THOMAS
THREE SHOWS 2 PM, 4 PM & 7 PM
WORLD FAMOUS WHITE BENGAL TIGERS
ADULTS ONLY

Magician Rick Thomas was one of the final performers in the Stardust show-room. His afternoon revue added an evening show in the summer of 2006. He shared the room with mind-reader Gerry McCambridge, "The Mentalist."

Night Club was delayed by a political drama of whether its cast would be granted exit visas from Cuba. The show eventually opened and played at the Stardust until February

2006. Three months after it debuted, its 43 performers filed for asylum petitions in Las Vegas. The revue was financially backed by Siegfried & Roy, who were close friends of producer Nicole Durr. Roy Horn's attendance at the show's premiere was his first public appearance after a near-fatal accident in October 2003, when a bite inflicted by one of the duo's show tigers led to a career-ending stroke.

As the Stardust showroom edged toward the finish line, the final headline act was likely to be the October dates of Steve Lawrence and Eydie Gorme, who also closed the legendary Circus Maximus showroom at Caesars Palace.

But many other venues at the Stardust featured entertainers of local and national renown over the years, helping the hotel-casino truly live up to its claim of being an entertainment mecca. Even the ballroom got into the act, with big bands, the male revue *Thunder From Down Under* and the female impersonator *Boy-Lesque* shows.

Bill Boyd remembers going there as a young man. "There was a lot of activity," he said. "It was an exciting place to be. Those were the days when large acts were the vogue in Las Vegas."

A Boyd favorite: *The Kim Sisters,* who performed in the Stardust lounge and also were featured on numerous national TV variety shows. He also liked *Brendan Boyer's Royal Irish Showband,* which was a popular attraction in the lounge during the 1960s and 1970s. The band was said to have a large and enthusiastic following, but one of its fans may be a bit surprising. Longtime employee Shirley Brancucci remembers that Elvis Presley liked to stop by the lounge to see Bowyer and the band perform.

"Elvis then was gorgeous," she says.

Havana Night Club brought full circle the link between casinos in pre-Castro Cuba and Las Vegas. The 2004 also brought Siegfried & Roy back to the Stardust, this time as producers, and generated headlines when its cast defected to the United States.

Beside the Garden Wall

A trip outside leads to speed, golf and excitement

Andy Williams draws a crowd at the 1968 Tony Lema Memorial Golf Tournament at the Stardust Country Club.

Relaxing Days

The Stardust had a well-deserved reputation as an entertainment center, but it offered plenty to do beyond the showrooms and lounge acts.

Auto racing, for example, at the Stardust International Raceway.

Golf, at the Stardust Country Club.

Equestrian events, at the Stardust Horsemans Park.

And sports, at various Stardust-sponsored sporting events conveniently cross-promoted with the Stardust Race & Sports Book, which was revolutionary for its time.

Some of the venues lasted longer than others, and not all were crammed onto the Stardust property near the north end of the Las Vegas Strip. But to Stardust long-timers, all were memorable.

"As a showgirl, you could donate your

All eyes are in the air to follow a Jack Nicklaus ball.

When he was still known as Cassius Clay, the boxing great Muhammad Ali was based at the Stardust while training for his 1965 fight with Floyd Patterson

time," said Rena Warden, who was with *Lido de Paris* from 1969 to 1979. She has photos of herself, in full showgirl regalia, at an appaloosa auction at the Stardust Horsemans Park — and remembers one horse who got a bit personal, first putting its nose in an upper private body part, and then in a lower private body part.

Horsemans Park, which was on the grounds west of the hotel, opened in 1967 and existed for more than 10 years.

Besides auctions, events included national horse shows, the Miss Rodeo America pageant, rodeos and various other events in the 500-seat arena complemented by 100 horse stalls.

The Stardust Country Club swung during the '60s, on a site four miles east of the hotel-casino on Desert Inn Road between Maryland Parkway and Eastern Avenue. Among the golfing greats who played in tournaments there

A young Chuck Norris proved he wasn't afraid of a girl when Debbie Reynolds chopped by for a publicity photo. Norris was training for his first-place victory at the Las Vegas National Karate Championships in 1969.

were Jack Nicklaus, Arnold Palmer and Don January, and a few entertainment greats, such as Andy Williams.

Exciting Days Too

A bit more unusual, as an amenity for a hotel-casino, was the Stardust International Raceway, which between 1965 and 1971 was located west of the Stardust, in an area that extended from Tropicana Avenue to Flamingo Road, bordered on one side by Rainbow Boulevard, the other by Piedmont Boulevard. Though it's difficult to believe now, looking at an overlay of the track on the present-day area, where single-family houses stand cheek-by-jowl on winding streets and cul-de-sacs, this was "way out there" in 1965; photos of the era show a

What's now a packed network of suburban streets once roared with the action of the Stardust International Raceway.

Parnelli Jones digs in for the 1967 Stardust CamAm race.

cleared spot in the desert with nothing but mountains visible in the background.

A 3-mile, "dead-level" track — sort of a crooked figure-eight — it also had a drag strip, stands, a concession area and "comfort stations."

The track was the site of many major races in its time, drawing such legendary names as "Big Daddy" Don Garlits, A.J. Foyt, Mario Andretti, Gordon Johncock, Al Unser, Bobby Unser, Parnelli Jones and Johnny Rutherford.

The track roared to life with ribbon-cutting ceremonies — the giant scissors wielded by Wilbur Clark and Moe Dalitz — on September 21, 1965. It immediately drew attention not only in the racing world but also in Hollywood. Lee Marvin was among the celebrities photographed at the 1965 Stardust Grand Prix. Bobby Unser took the first-place trophy in a 1968 Indy Car Race, and Stirling Moss competed in the 1967 Stardust Grand Prix, which was won by John Surtees.

And as always, the resort used its assets to help promote its other assets. A *Lido de Paris* showgirl was photographed in 1968 as she prepared to take off around the track on a dirt bike.

But let's not forget the resort's restaurants,

SURTEES WINS STARDUST GRAND PRIX

FINALE TO CAN-AM SERIES CLIMAXES SIX THRILLING RACING EVENTS

SURTEES WINS STARDUST GRAND PRIX

SURTEES
Double Victory

A determined young man from Surrey, England, John Surtees led every lap and ran away with both the Stardust Grand Prix and the coveted overall Canadian-American Challenge Cup Series in record time.

Driving a Lola T-70 Chevrolet, Surtees had an average race speed of 109.25 mph, breaking the old record of 106.68 held by Hap Sharp.

OFF AND RUNNING!

John Surtees (left #7), Jim Hall (#66) and Jackie Stewart (#43) head into Turn One at the beginning of the 210-mile Stardust Grand Prix. Surtees led at the end of the first lap and then proceeded to pull away. In addition to the G.P. and Can-Am prize money, Surtees got paid $50 for each of the 70 laps, all of which he led.

JOHN SURTEES broke both the race lap and average speed records at the Stardust Grand Prix when he drove his Lola T-70 to victory and captured the Can-Am Challenge Cup Series as well.

Competitors chased the thrill of victory from a 1,000-foot platform to the Stardust swimming pool in the World High Diving Championships, televised by ABC's Wide World of Sports in 1965.

149

Throughout the years, the Stardust offered a wide variety of food and beverage styles. Below, restaurant menus from Moby Dick and a photo of the restaurant entrance. Opposite: Menus from Toucan Harry's, Ralph's Diner, Tres Lobos and at far right, a beverage menu from Lido de Paris.

some of which became legends unto themselves. Aku Aku, which was open from 1960 to 1980, must have seemed downright exotic during the earlier part of that period. Touting a menu of "Polynesian" food (but known mostly for its umbrella drinks, including one served in a pineapple), it announced itself with huge lava statues resembling those on Easter Island.

"Aku Aku was the place to go," said William S. 'Bill' Boyd, chairman and CEO of Boyd Gaming, who remembers visiting the Stardust as a young man. "It had a bridge that you walked over. That was kind of exciting in those days."

The seafood restaurant was the Moby Dick, where Carol Geraci, a diminutive Stardust cocktail waitress who worked there from 1966 until the closing in 2006, remembers being asked to sit on Jimmy Durante's lap.

"I was so excited," Geraci said. "He was the sweetest man."

150

Other Stardust restaurants included The Palm Room, The Royal Beef Room, the Plantation Kitchen, Tony Roma's (not the one where Lefty Rosenthal's car was blown up), The Warehouse Buffet, Coco Palms, William B's, Sushi King, Toucan Harry's, Tres Lobos and Ralph's Diner, a salute to the great '50s diners, complete with period-costumed servers and a jukebox full of oldies.

A Taste of the Good Life

Aku Aku would've been tough to miss when it opened in January 1960. Massive — upwards of 30-foot — heads in the style of the Easter Island statues marked its entrance, and one was right out on Las Vegas Boulevard.

The heads and much of the rest of the restaurant's décor had been created by Californian Eli Hedley, who found a certain measure of fame as the world's first "beachcomber" and brought the essence of the islands

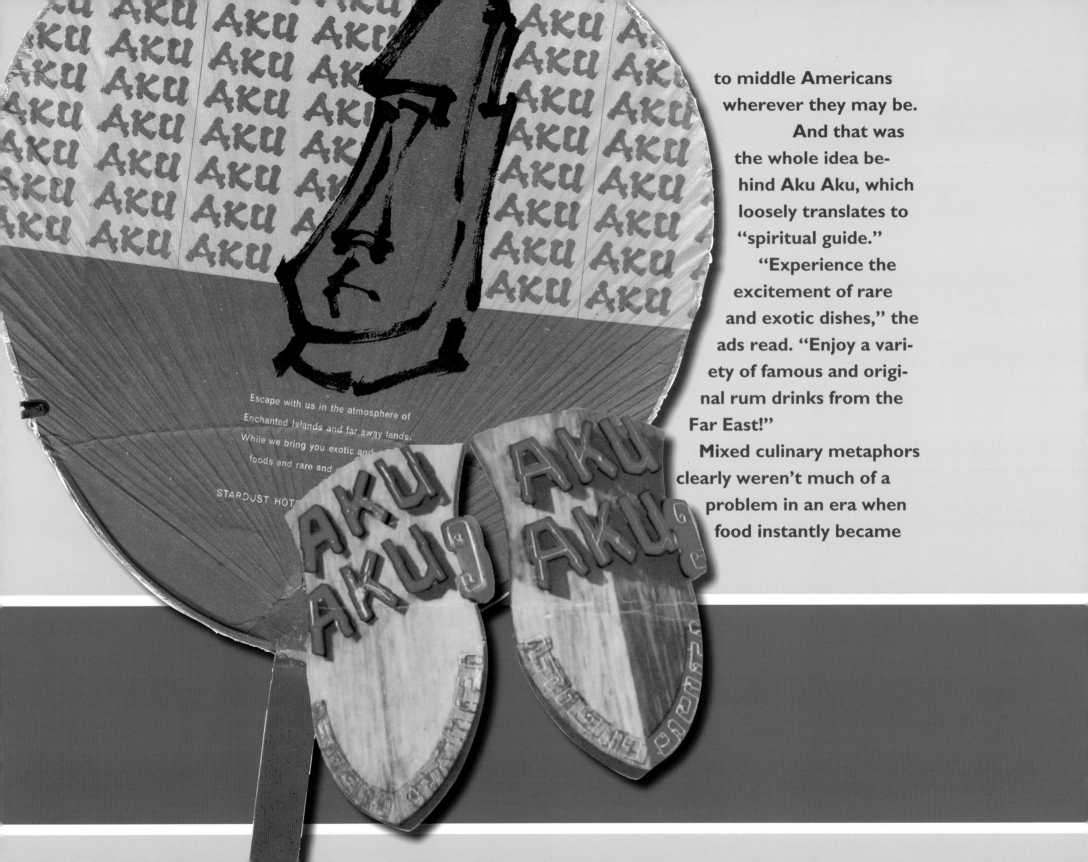

Escape with us in the atmosphere of
Enchanted Islands and far away lands.
While we bring you exotic and
foods and rare and

STARDUST HOT

to middle Americans wherever they may be. And that was the whole idea behind Aku Aku, which loosely translates to "spiritual guide." "Experience the excitement of rare and exotic dishes," the ads read. "Enjoy a variety of famous and original rum drinks from the Far East!"

Mixed culinary metaphors clearly weren't much of a problem in an era when food instantly became

"Polynesian" with the addition of a pine-apple ring. And while rum isn't generally thought of in connection with the Far East, that didn't really matter either. The whole "tiki" craze was less about authenticity than about domesticating a taste of the South Seas life American servicemen had experienced during their tours of duty.

Aku Aku's drinks were created at least in part by Don Beach, the Don the Beach-comber who had a place of his own over at the Sahara. And what drinks they were; oh-so-sweet mixtures served up in elabo-rate style in vessels so iconic that today they're collectors' items.

There was the Aku Aku Gold Cup, a stemmed glass contain-ing its own little bandshell

of crushed ice cooling "Mexican limes" (much more exotic in the pre-NAFTA era). And the Savage Island Pearl Cock-tail, "especially recom-mended for ladies" with "a genuine pearl in each cock-tail." And all for $1.20. And don't forget the Shark's Tooth, whose main at-tribute seemed to be the shards of ice rimming the glass that sub-tly evoked shark teeth.

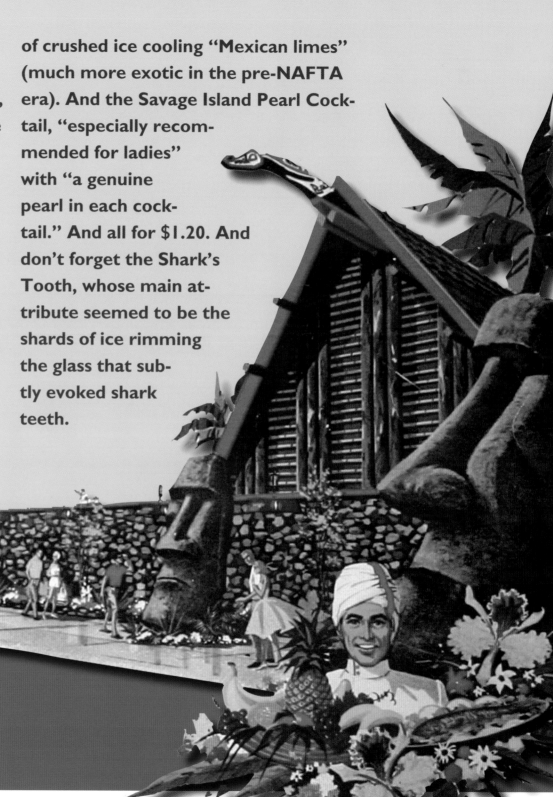

Aku Aku closed in 1980, a victim of changing tastes; Tiki-themed restaurants all but died out in the mainstream, passing the torch to a devout cult following. Eli Hedley's grandson has followed in the family business and creates tiki bars under the name Bamboo Ben, with an eponymous shop in Huntington Beach, California.

A coconut-shaped drinking vessel inscribed with the Aku Aku name recently sold for $67.77 on e-Bay.

And of the iconic heads, which Hedley

ORIGINAL DRINKS

AKU-AKU GOLD CUP
A mixture of Mexican limes, Cuban syrup, Jamaican rhum, Puerto Rican rhum and dashes of almond and herbsaint.
1.25

SAVAGE ISLAND PEARL COCKTAIL
Especially recommended for ladies.
A genuine pearl in each cocktail.
1.20

CHERRY BLOSSOM
A delicate rhum punch combining haunting flavors of the Orient and reminiscent of cherry blossom time on the slopes of Fujiyama, topped with a petite Japanese parasol.
1.00

MAI KAI SWIZZLE
Blend of tropical fruit juices and herbs with old Jamaican rhums, Puerto Rican and Barbados rhums. Garnished with fresh Hawaiian pineapple, maraschino cherry and fresh garden mint.
1.75

SCORPION
Minimum of two persons per bowl. This drink is refreshing and mellow, but has the effect of a scorpion bite. Floated with fresh Belmont gardenia.
1.75 For one   Limit 4 per bowl

ORIGINAL DRINKS   from the FAR ISLANDS

BARREL OF RHUM
Combination of West Indies rhums and tropical fruit juices and herbs.
1.50
take the barrel home 3.00

CON TECCI COCONUT
Coconut milk mixed with rhums from Martinique and fruit juices from the tropics.
1.50
ke the coconut shell home 3.00

MANA COCKT...
...(FLY)
This drink of velvety ...
taste with the satisfyi...
will bring back your ...
to start drinking ag...
...25

PLANTER'S PUNCH JAMAICA, Jamaican rhum base 1.00
PLANTER'S PUNCH CUBA, mixed with Cuban rhum .. 1.00
PLANTER'S PUNCH TRINIDAD, Trinidad rhum 1.10
PLANTER'S PUNCH DEMERARA, Demerara rhum 1.20
PLANTER'S PUNCH MARTINIQUE, Martinique rhum 1.10

MANACURA COFFEE GROGG
Satisfying, delicious, beautiful
1.50

CAPTAIN COOK'S GROGG
Specially recommended for those who fancy themselves explorers.
1.75

AKU-AKU DAIQUIRI
A mellow white rhum, juice of Acapulco limes and a touch of white syrup. A superbly blended cocktail.
1.00

SHARK'S TOOTH
A cocktail with a bite like a shark, a house-broken shark.
1.25

FOG CUTTER
This drink will vanish the foggy days in your future.
1.75 For one   Limit 2 per bowl

TABU SWIZZLE
A very nourishing and potent creation served in bamboo glass. Combination of rhums, herbs and spices and fruit juices.
1.50
Take the glass home 2.00

ORIGINAL DRINKS   from

ROYAL AKU TIKI
The image (Guardian Angel) symbolizes the Easter Island legend. The drink is a mixture of exotic fruit juices and rhums from the West Indies and Puerto Rico.
Take home the mug 2.25

BROWN TIKI
This is the original Tiki. (means God in Polynesian)
This drink is one of our original concoctions. It tastes different but it is refreshing.
Take home the mug 2.25

PUKA PO-'O
(Hole in the Head)
The name sounds scary but the drink will quench your thirst and give you a delightful feeling.
Take home the mug 3.50

PUA-PULE
(Flower on a Shell)
This is a very romantic setting for lovers. A kiss after each quaff will put you in the mood for love.
3.50

HURRICANE
This blend of fruit juices and different rhums will give you a lift and throw you into a whirl of exotic fantasy.
2.00

RHU...
A very ...
flavoure...
and aro...

MOON ANI...
A far island ...
Maui Limes, H...
and Guava Nec...

LADY PRE...
A semi frozen ...
will aid digesti...

AR ISLANDS

rhum,
mint

2.00

DR. WING
It's licorice, but it will stir the warmth
of your blood to a height
culminating in splendor.

1.25

on,

1.00

RANGOON RUBY
A very light and delicate cocktail
that will sparkle your evening.

1.25

sM

1.25

carved of volcanic featherstone rock? The fate of one remains unknown. But one was donated to Clark County and remains at Sunset Park, on Sunset Road in the south part of the valley.

On an island, of course.

ORIGINAL DRINKS

from the FAR ISLANDS

MAI TAI
A very popular drink along Waikiki Beach because of its well balanced taste.
1.75

COL. PLANTATION PUNCH
You will find that this hearty rhum punch will give you comfort, warm your blood and restore your strength.
1.75

BORA BORA SWIZZLE
British Guiana Demerara rhum.
151 proof is subtly combined with tropical fruit juices.
This is not recommended for non-drinkers.
Take home the mug 3.00
2.50
Take home the mug 3.00

BARBADOS PUNCH
Rhums from the islands of Barbados, mixed with fresh fruit juices, this drink will disperse the clouds of care.
1.75

SLIGHTLY BITTEN
Lifts one's spirit and heals the bite.
Limit of 3 bites per guest.
1.50

PARADISE PUNCH
This creation was in the finals at the 1961 Early Times National Drink Contest. It is a blend of bourbon with sweet and sour fresh lime juice and apricot liqueur.
1.25

AKU AKU RUMBLE
The juice of luscious golden Hawaiian pineapple blended with rhums from Jamaica and the Barbados makes this drink mysterious, reminiscent of an eruption of a Hawaiian volcano.
1.50

AKU AKU LAPU
Magellan – discoverer of the Philippines was killed by Lapu-Lapu.
We recommend this drink to those who fancy themselves as warriors of the 16th Century.
2.00 Single 4.00 Double

SHIP OF FLAME
This delicious cocktail will fan the flames of love to a white heat.
1.25

EASTER ISLAND SWIZZLE
As mysterious as the Island of the Long Ears and the Short Ears.
You have to try this drink for curiosity's sake.
2.50 Single 5.00 Double

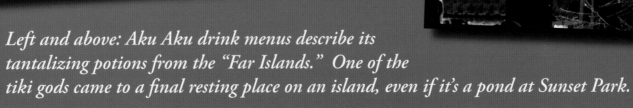

Left and above: Aku Aku drink menus describe its tantalizing potions from the "Far Islands." One of the tiki gods came to a final resting place on an island, even if it's a pond at Sunset Park.

Twilight Time

An extended family faces the end of a legend

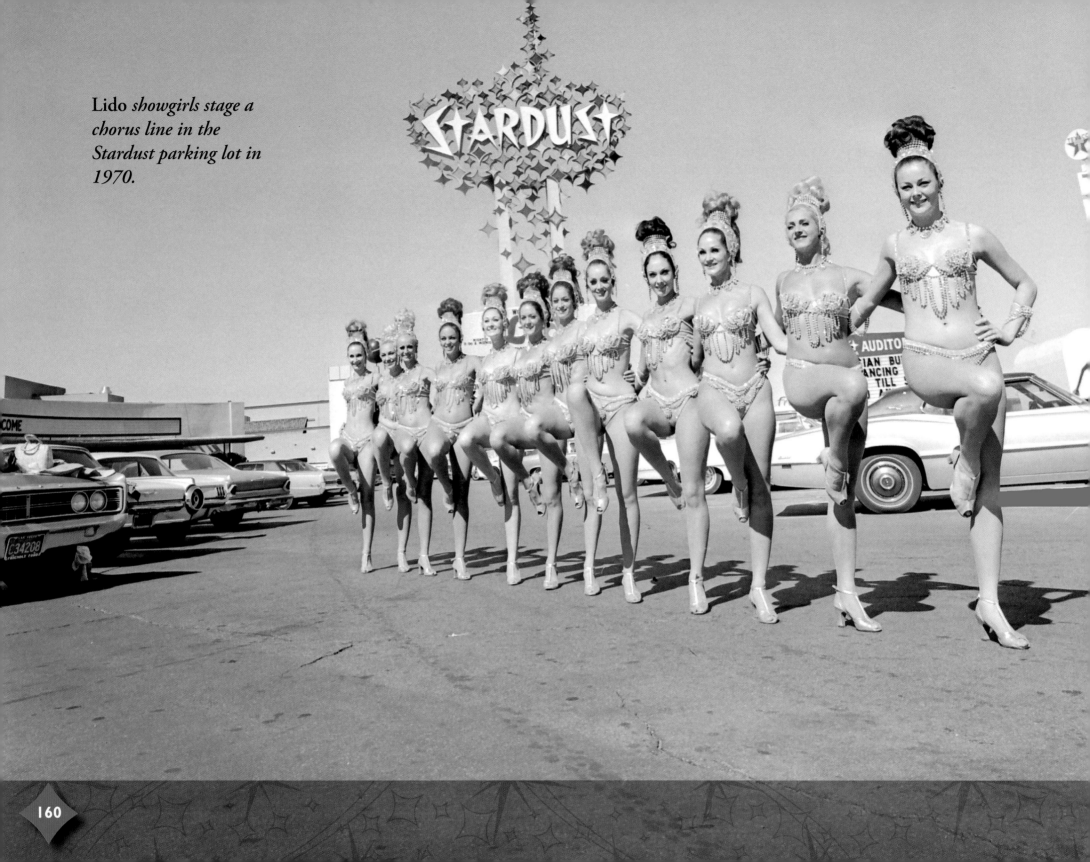

Lido *showgirls stage a chorus line in the Stardust parking lot in 1970.*

One Big Family

As 2006 comes to a close, the Stardust's lights won't be glowing on the Las Vegas Strip for the first time in nearly 50 years. The dusty construction site that Bill Boyd remembers from the mid-'50s will be back in a new context while the mammoth Echelon Place becomes reality.

But the venerable Stardust will be far from forgotten.

"Most of our customers now are upset that it's not going to be the Stardust," said Shirley Brancucci, longtime employee and baccarat pit boss. "They say, 'We don't come to Las Vegas; we come to the Stardust.'"

And repeatedly, they stress the friendliness of the staff, the commitment to service.

George Havlik of Kimball, South Dakota, and his wife, Judy, went to the Stardust for "in the neighborhood of 28 years." All three of their sons and three of their grandsons have

Veteran Stardust employees, from left to right: Tom McEwen, Shirley Brancucci, Carol Geraci and Len Rader, and Len's wife, Jill, who performed in Lido de Paris *in 1959.*

been there as well.

"It's just like going home," Havlik said. "They always took good care of us. It's really been quite a place. You get to know so many people from all over the country."

Lucille Waughsmith of Lakewood, Colorado, said she went to the Stardust for 25 years, beginning when her husband was alive. They initially were drawn to the hotel-casino because their son, Tony Smith, worked there. But while Smith moved on after 13 years, Waughsmith kept coming back, "because I like it. I like the ambiance. I like the friendly people. I like it because it's homey." At the new megaresorts, "you can get lost in 5 minutes. You can't get lost (at the Stardust). And if people want to find you, they can.

"Everybody knows that Vegas is to take your money. It's how it's taken that counts — if it's taken with a friendly smile. I appreciate the fact that after 25 years, everybody does know me and treats me very cordially. I hope I never take advantage of it. Everything I need is at my fingertips."

Waughsmith was so close to the Stardust, she knew many of the employees.

"That includes right down to the housekeeper, Petra," she said. Her favorite waiter was Jorge Perreira, "who was married to Miss Mexico of 1960." And of course her favorite hostess, Linda Colvin.

"There's no vying to take clients" among hosts and hostesses, Waughsmith said. "And I like that."

Donald and Patty Fiscus of Cape Coral, Florida, have visited the Stardust an average of five times a year since they started going there in 1990. The reason? "How well we were treated and the friendliness of the people," he said.

Ursula Stehn of Arlington, Texas, first stayed at the Stardust because her husband, who worked for American Airlines, was offered a special package.

On their next visit to Las Vegas, they returned to the Stardust. But when they arrived, they were told that their reservations couldn't be found.

"I said, 'Oh, great; we have no place to stay,' " Stehn remembers.

A casino hostess overheard.

"She said, 'Is there a problem? You just wait; I'll find someplace for you to put your heads.' "

"From then on, we kept on going back to the Stardust," Stehn said. "It got to be like a family affair. The people got to be like friends; they weren't employees. It's a personal thing. They inquire, 'How's your son? How's your daughter?' It's not like it is in so many places, where you're just a number."

The Stehns ended up visiting monthly, sometimes twice a month.

"All of a sudden somebody will be in back of you and hug you from the back," Stehn said. "Where do you get that kind of individual attention?"

Just as Boyd Gaming worked to

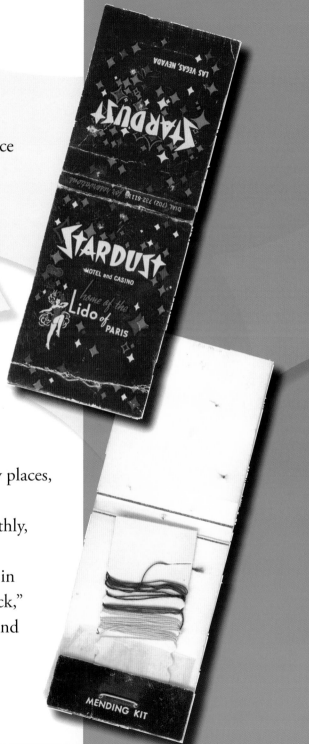

Architectural critic Alan Hess called the original Stardust "a parking lot with a sign," a forerunner of strip-mall design that later became known as a "decorated shed."

The space-age display was designed by Kermit Wayne, who had worked as a scenic artist for movie studios and as a sign-painter before joining the Young Electric Sign Company (YESCO) in 1957.

A press release for the hotel's opening correctly predicted the future importance of the façade: "It will undoubtedly prove to be one of the most photographed items in the Las Vegas area." Facts and figures about the sign have varied, but the original press release said it was 216 feet long, 37 feet high and weighed 129 tons. It used 7,100 feet of neon tubing and 11,000 incandescent lamps.

By 1965, the Strip was all

Above and opposite right: The Stardust's new outdoor sign in 1991 dropped the futuristic logo that had carried through from the earliest days. Right, Paul Miller's 1965 replacement for the original round sign, opposite left, cost $500,000 in 1965.

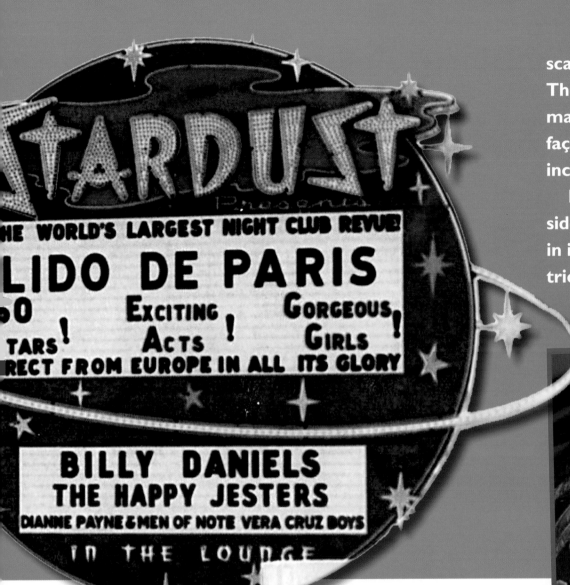

scaled to beckon the highway motorist. The Stardust responded with a roadside marquee that adapted the original building façade but animated it with both neon and incandescent bulbs.

In 1991, the hotel made what many consider to be the one of the worst mistakes in its history, replacing the distinctive electric lettering with a sans-serif Helvetica.

The following images are taken from a 1968 portfolio of Stardust accommodations. Above: Typical Galaxy and Chateau rooms priced between $19 and $30 per night. Middle: Executive Suite Parlor, 9th floor Galaxy Building priced between $70 and $75 per night. Right: Presidential Penthouse Suite (Parlor) priced between $75 and $82 per night.

Left: Chateau Deluxe Suite Poolside Parlor priced between $60 and $65 per night offered an upstairs bedroom. Middle and Right: Two design options for the Stardust Satellite. This room was only $12 to $17 per night.

find other places for employees who wanted to stay with the company, so they worked with their guests, Bill Boyd said.

"We're giving guests tours of our other properties," Boyd said. "Tours of all possibilities, so they could choose which one suits them the best.

"It's very emotional for lifetime guests. They almost have tears in their eyes: 'Why do you want to take it away from us?'

"That's the price of progress. You have to move on in order to compete."

Boyd said many longtime guests wanted memorabilia — tangible pieces of the Stardust — and attempts were being made to accommodate those requests.

Stehn said many of her Stardust friends were bereft as the closing neared, with some vowing that they wouldn't even return to Las Vegas.

"I don't think we'll ever find a place in Las Vegas like the Stardust," she said.

Many other longtime guests say they plan to move their gaming to the Orleans, a Boyd property on West Tropicana Avenue.

"I kind of started that ball rolling," Waughsmith said with a chuckle.

"That's where some of the Stardust people went," Fiscus said. "We likely will stay there."

"Wherever our hostess goes, that's where we'll go," Stehn said.

"I made it very clear that the three main hostesses needed to be in the Orleans," Waughsmith said.

She also was pushing for the Orleans to implement limousine service. "They're gonna have to make some changes," she said. "People over there aren't very accepting of changes, but that's tough luck."

Looking Back, Looking Forward

One of the changes most lamented by longtime guests is the demise of the Stardust name.

"I know they just have to keep growing," Stehn said, but "they should not do away with that name. The New Stardust or whatever. Something to keep that name alive. They're losing the old Las Vegas completely. But I guess

A Long Stopover

Carol Geraci didn't plan to become a cocktail waitress. And when she did, her family wasn't exactly happy about it.

She was a native of Superior, Arizona; population: Not much (maybe 3,200). By 1966, she was ready to get out and lined up a job in Santa Barbara, California.

But on the way, she stopped in Las Vegas. Eddie Haddad, from her hometown, owned and operated the Mexican restaurant Macayo Vegas. He asked if she wouldn't rather stay in town and be a cocktail waitress. "He sent me down to the union the next day, and I had a job at the Pioneer Club downtown," she recalls. "I didn't want to come downtown. I wanted to go home to Mama."

After a few months working at the Pioneer under the iconic neon sign Vegas Vic, she moved to the Stardust and worked there until it closed.

Geraci admits to being naïve. "I came from Arizona and didn't know what the mob was."

Over the years, she thoroughly enjoyed the friendships she made on the job.

"Where could you go every day," she said, "and you make good money and meet good people — even if they're losing money?"

Carol Geraci was a cocktail waitress at the Stardust from 1966 until the casino closed in 2006.

The late Sam Boyd, left, and son Bill took the Stardust from mob control to the era of corporate financing. Boyd Gaming is the third-largest casino corporation.

we don't have anything to say about that. This big corporation is going to talk about that."

"It's not because we don't have great feelings for the Stardust," Boyd said. The change, he said, is necessary because "we're going to do something so different." Echelon Place, he said, is a "name that will denote what we're going to be creating on the Stardust site."

That will include 63 acres with the 2,600-room Resort Tower and 700-suite Suite Tower. Two spas, one million square feet of exhibition and meeting space, a 4,000-seat theater and a 1,500-seat theater. More than 25 restaurants and bars. Elaborately landscaped pools. A retail promenade. And three more hotels: one from the Hong Kong-based Shangri-La Hotels and Resorts group, plus a Delano hotel and a Mondrian hotel from the Morgans Hotel Group, each with their own additional amenities. All of

STARDUST NEWS

MISS 1967

Merry Christmas Happy New

"STARDUST means extra excitement"

Before they were famous: Goldie Hawn was a cover model for the Christmas 1967 issue of Stardust News, a pioneer in direct marketing to frequent hotel guests. Valerie Perrine was a Lido showgirl and posed for a Stardust publicity photo before achieving movie acclaim in Lenny.

it scheduled to open in 2010.

And if longtime guests are concerned about the presence of familiar faces, they may be somewhat comfortable to know that Bob Boughner will lead the development of the project as president and

Over the years, cheesecake and showcards became a recurring promotional tool at the Stardust.

chief executive officer of Echelon Resorts.

Bill Boyd said Boughner started as a timekeeper, punching time cards downtown at the California in 1975. He became a cook and kept moving up, at one point serving as an assistant general manager at the Stardust. Boughner's most recent post was in Atlantic City, where he was president and chief operating officer of Borgata, the company's inspiration for Echelon Place.

Boyd also is enthusiastic about what he sees as the resurgence of the north end of the Strip.

"The north end used to be the center of activity," he said. "This is where all the action was in those days.

"I think it is the future of the Strip in Las Vegas. Starting with Wynn Las Vegas, what we're going to do with Echelon, the Frontier, Rivera and another opportunity across from the Riviera. Someday the greatest resorts are going to be on the north end of the Strip."

Terry Lovern, who has helped run entertainment at the Stardust for years, enters the backstage dressing room with a headdress from the final edition of Lido de Paris.

"Lido de Paris"
1977

The Memory

Even Bill Boyd gets a little wistful as he talks about the Stardust.

"We've really enjoyed it," he said. "It's been a wonderful place to own."

"Look honey, nobody likes change," frequent visitor Lucille Waughsmith said. "But you're always going to have that. You're sad about it; there's no question. But you also know that times change and if you don't keep up with them, you'll get lost in the dust."

Of Echelon Place, she said, "It's going to be very large. It's going to be uncomfortable.

"Until you get used to it."

"I'll miss it so much," said Shirley Brancucci, who still worked two days a week in the pit, at age 77, when the Stardust closed "We're friends. We go to dinner. I've made so many friendships over the years."

"I'll still have coffee with customers who come to town," Carol Geraci said. "It's not about money. It's about friendship."

"That's how they are," Brancucci said of casino guests. "They think about you."

"It's been a great job," Geraci said. "It's been quite a ride. The whole thing."

"It's been, like you said, a great ride," Brancucci said.

"It has."

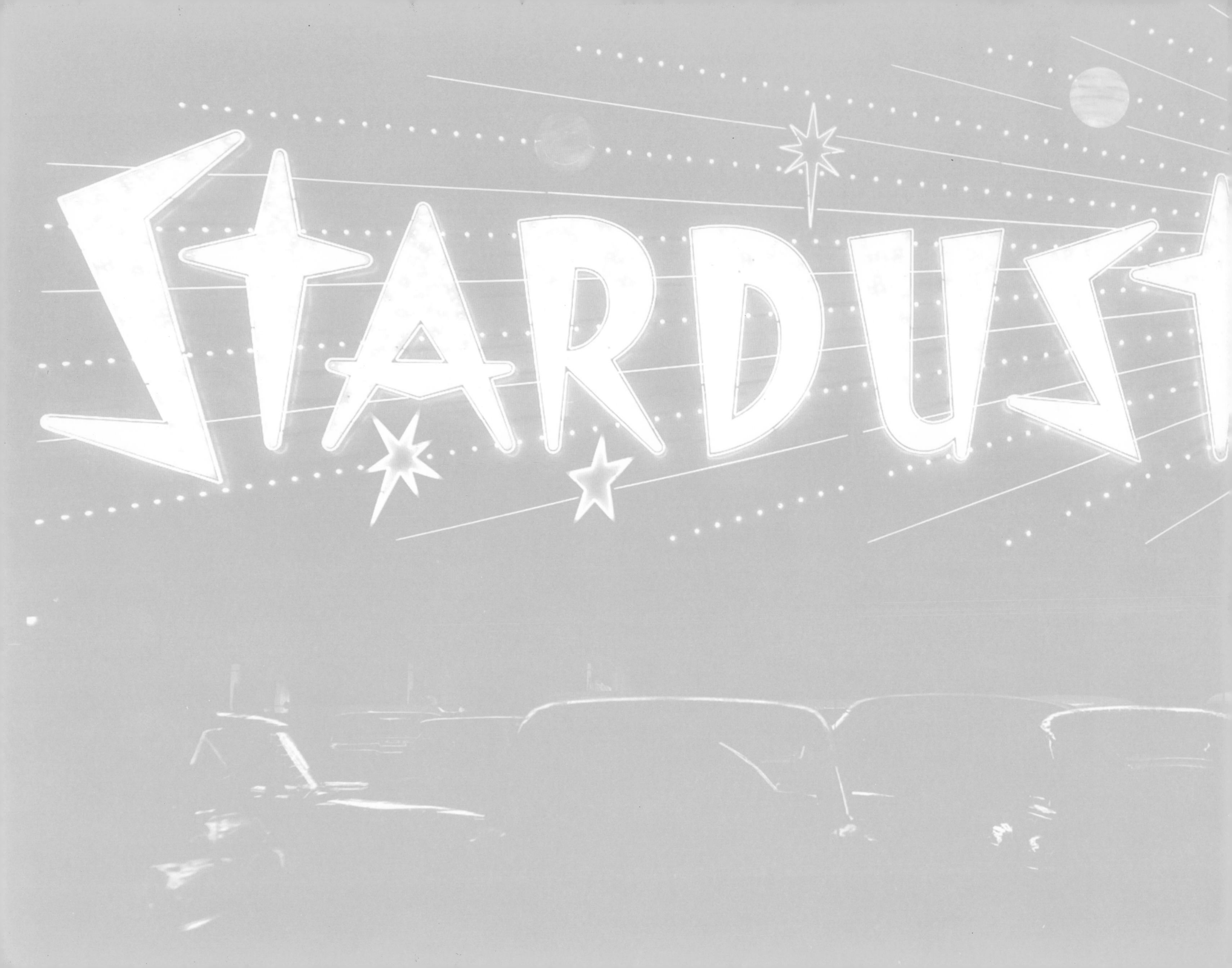
STARDUST